LECKHAMPTON
YESTERYEAR

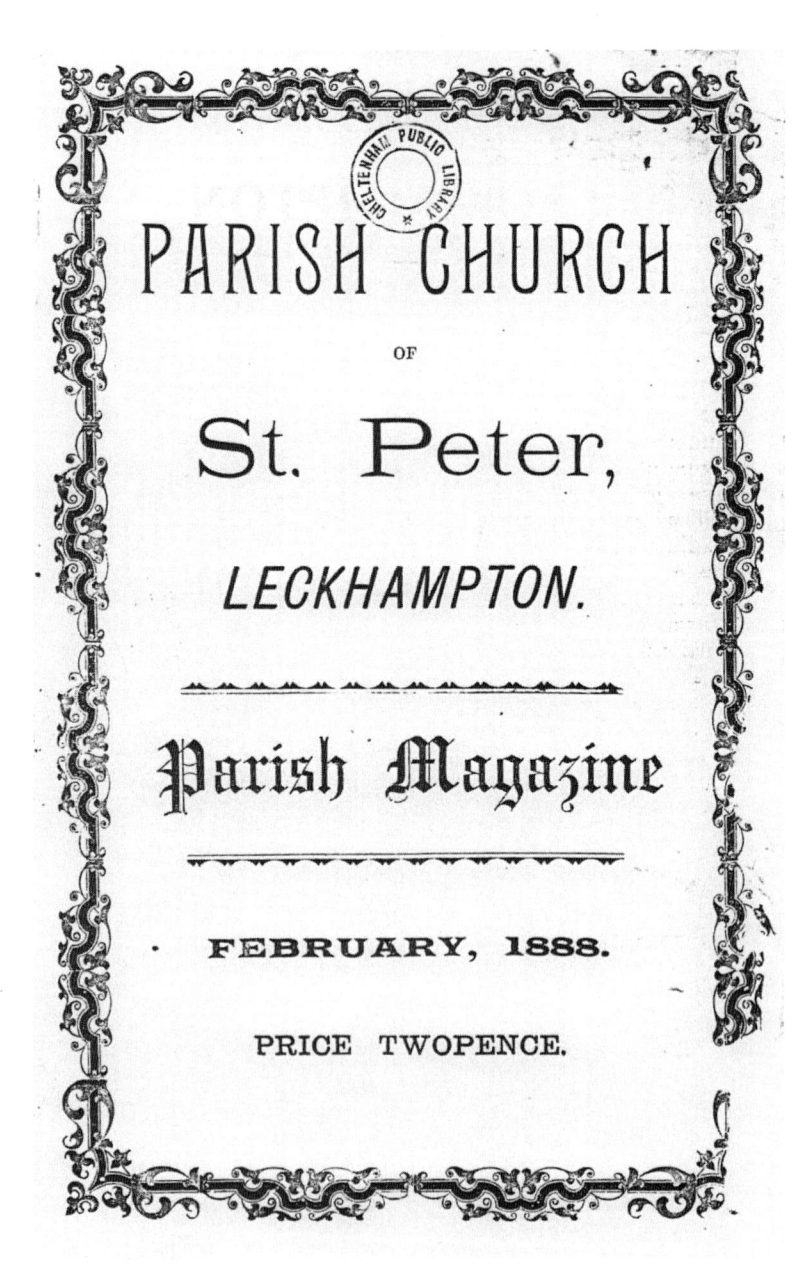

PARISH CHURCH

OF

St. Peter,

LECKHAMPTON.

𝕻arish 𝕸agazine

FEBRUARY, 1888.

PRICE TWOPENCE.

Cover of the first issue of the
Leckhampton Parish Magazine

LECKHAMPTON YESTERYEAR

*

Leckhampton Local History Society

Leckhampton

Saint  Peter

Parish Messenger

Drawing of St Peter's Church as used on the cover of the
Leckhampton Parish Messenger, 1920 to1939

LECKHAMPTON YESTERYEAR

VILLAGE LIFE, 1888 - 1939

ERIC MILLER

*

Leckhampton Local History Society

By the same author

The History of Leckhampton Church

Leckhampton in the Second World War (joint editor)

Britain in Old Photographs – Leckhampton (with Alan Gill)

Leckhampton Court – Manor House to Hospice

The Stained-glass Windows of Leckhampton Church

Cover illustration: Watercolour by T Cole, fl 1883, showing Collum End Farm and the church spire, based on an earlier lithograph by Joseph Powell, published in his *Liber Naturalis,* 1824.
(Private collection)

ISBN 978 0 9524200 7 1

First printed 1996
Revised and reprinted by Mixam Printing, Watford, 2021
Typesetting by the author

Published by the Leckhampton Local History Society
www.llhs.org.uk

CONTENTS

Dedicated to the past inhabitants of Leckhampton,
who made this book possible

*

'The *Parish Messengers* make very interesting reading. Not only are they a detailed and consecutive history of our church and parish life ... but they necessarily refer occasionally to external and even international events, showing what kind of impact they made on Leckhampton; and, what is more, they reflect very clearly the thoughts, sentiments, ideas, customs and needs of their time. It is fascinating to see how these things change rather subtly and almost imperceptibly from year to year ... Above all, they demonstrate, beyond all doubt, what is abiding and what is ephemeral in our church life.'

The Reverend Paul Dack, in 1955, when Curate at Leckhampton

*

In the years covered by this book, the Parish Magazines were edited by the following priests:

1885-1895	Reginald Edward Trye
1895-1904	William Clifford Aston
1904-1912	Henry Proctor
1912-1915	Frederick William Bidwell
1915-1921	Augustine (Austin) John Hodson
1921-1928	Francis Reginald Standfast
1928-1938	Frederick William Sears
1938-1940	Henry James Hensman

FOREWORD

When I was carrying out my research for *The History of Leckhampton Church,* the Parish Magazines were among my sources. I soon realised that they also contained some fascinating accounts of other matters, which may have been too parochial and ephemeral to be recorded elsewhere, but which have taken on an added significance with the passage of time, and I felt that these discoveries deserved to be shared with a wider audience.

It may be thought that the articles in a church magazine would have been limited in scope and inclined to view the world through rose-tinted spectacles, and also that a chronicle of events in *Leckhampton Yesteryear* would be more complete if a variety of other sources were used as well. On the contrary, there is ample awareness of the wider world and of both local and national life, including its darker side. The church was at the heart of community life, and many local projects and activities of all kinds were initiated by the Rector and overseen by his parishioners. This is reflected in the magazines, and I particularly wish to show that, as a collection, these have a distinctive character of their own.

The magazines first appeared in 1888, and I have concentrated on events from then to the start of the Second World War, which may be regarded as the heyday of the magazine, and perhaps of the village too: before the motor car and aeroplane had become commonplace, when a train journey even to Bishops Cleeve was both a major undertaking and a special treat, and when people made their own entertainment and charades and magic lantern shows thrilled young and old alike. These accounts provide an insight into the attitudes of what was still a largely rural community, with a strong individual identity, looking after its own welfare. I believe that the Leckhampton magazines, in common with many others that were emerging at about the same time, reflect the social history not only of Leckhampton and Cheltenham but also of England itself.

I have occasionally included information from other sources, but only where required for clarity or completeness. On the other hand, I have avoided needless duplication of accounts that are to be found in other published works.

I have for the most part written the book as a narrative and have only quoted word for word where I felt that it was necessary to convey the precise flavour of the original article. Elsewhere it should be apparent where I have summarised or paraphrased or added an explanatory comment. It should particularly be noted that those writing some hundred years ago sometimes used racist language and expressed discriminatory attitudes that would be unacceptable today. To omit such instances, however, would give a false impression of the times.

The factual accounts may strike chords with others who are familiar with the village in years past and should be a useful starting point for anyone wishing to embark on a more general history of the area or with an interest in the life of the period.

A number of alterations and additions have been made to the original text for this revised edition, to take account of more recent developments and also in the light of my own research during the past 25 years. Many of the illustrations are new for this edition and have been taken from the Local History Society's collection unless otherwise stated.

My thanks are due to past Rectors of Leckhampton, to the staff of Cheltenham Local and Family History Centre and to the late Miss Jean Bendall for enabling me to see surviving copies of the early magazines.

I also thank the committee of the Leckhampton Local History Society for agreeing to underwrite the republication of this book. The original book was printed by the late Reverend George Smith after he had retired to Bledington.

I also express my thanks to my wife for her encouragement and for her help and advice over the editing and proofreading.

Eric Miller
20 Collum End Rise

Revised April 2021

Chapter One
THE PARISH MAGAZINE

THE 'PARISH MESSENGER'

Right from the beginning the Parish Magazine was intended as a monthly record of local news, and for many years, until 1968, it was known as the 'Leckhampton Parish Messenger'. In the first issue of February 1888 the Reverend R E Trye wrote:

> 'My dear friends!
>
> 'I have for a long time thought that it would be a very good thing if we could have a Parish Magazine, and now I am determined ... to carry out my desire.
>
> 'It is proposed to give a Monthly Record of our Parish News, also of Baptisms, Marriages and Funerals. Thus it will be a kind of Parish Register, and will be useful for us all to refer to as a record of what has taken place from year to year.
>
> 'Besides the Local News of the Month there will be other matter ... so I trust you will give a hearty welcome to what will be our Parish Magazine. Take it in yourselves, and introduce it to your friends, so that it may be a regular Monthly Record of Leckhampton News.
>
> Your Friend and Pastor,
>
> R E Trye'

Many of Reginald Trye's successors were equally conscientious and, what is more, took steps to have copies of the magazine bound and held in safe-keeping. It is thanks to their foresight that a reasonably complete set of magazines still exists.

By 1898 160 copies were sold each month, priced at three old pence, but from January 1918 they were issued free. Later on advertisements brought in some revenue, though this did not cover the cost of production. A proposal to reintroduce a charge was dropped and in 1924 the printing was instead transferred from Burrow's Press to Geo Hooper, of 19a Suffolk Parade. In a tribute to Burrow's, the Rector commented 'excellent work, none better (though others may print more cheaply)'.

The standard of appearance was high. In an age of letter press, the typography was attractive and varied in style, and any odd spaces were filled with ornamental scrolls typical of their period (some of which I have reproduced in this book). When clergyman had servants and fewer commitments outside their parish, they could devote time to editing and proofreading. Typographical errors were rare, and the few 'howlers' (British *Guano* Mission for British Guiana Mission, for example) stand out as rare exceptions.

There was always an introductory letter written by the Rector, which varied in tone according to individual preoccupations and the state of the world around and was by no means confined to religious matters. As clubs and societies were formed, their activities were reported, and the villagers' outings and entertainments are now of especial interest. In some cases these reports were reprinted from one of the local newspapers, and there were also occasional special articles.

THE PARISH REGISTER

The core of the magazine was (as it still is) the 'Parish Register' to which Reginald Trye alluded: lists of services and forthcoming events, names and addresses of officials and others responsible for organising parish activities, and particulars of baptisms, marriages and burials, including the ages of the deceased. Among other things, this Register now serves as a useful directory of those who were active in the village over the period in question. (An example is reproduced opposite.)

In the early Parish Registers the number of baptisms ranged between seven and twenty a year, but comparatively few marriages were recorded (from two to seven). The number of burials was surprisingly high (73 in 1890, for example) even allowing for the fact that at that time parishioners of St Philip and St James's had the right to be buried in the churchyard. In 1904 it was remarked that of the 50 burials, only 12 were of former residents of the parish. More died in infancy or childhood than nowadays, but on the other hand there were plenty who reached the ripe old age of 80 or more.

In 1889, eight of those buried had died in infancy but seven were over 80. Out of 100 burials in 1892, 20 occurred in January. In 1910 the Reverend Henry Proctor wrote that 'the average age of the last thirteen persons buried in our churchyard (excluding one child of 5 years) is over 86 years and 6 months'.

𝔓arish 𝔐essenger.

A page from a *Parish Messenger* of 1920

The numbers fluctuated, but some comparative figures are shown in the table below:

	Baptisms	Marriages	Burials	(aged over 80)
1929	12	7	48	9
1935	16	8	38	10
1937	26	11	43	12
1946	36	20	40	12

Further comments were sometimes added. One of these indicates the stability of the population in earlier years. In 1896, William Hicks, late of Collum End Farm, who died at the age of 81, was described as 'till recently, perhaps the most familiar figure in Leckhampton, where he had resided all his life, never having left it except for a fortnight on one occasion'.

Other obituaries are summarised more appropriately elsewhere in this book, but one headed *Our Village Doctor*, deserves a mention here. It honours Dr Harold Lloyd Davies, who died in 1920 and after whom the surgery in Moorend Park Road is named.

'Everybody knew him: not a dog which did not welcome him at a home of sickness; not a child whom he did not assist to make its first bow in this strange and wonderful world; hardly a traveller on his way out of it for whom he has not eased the journey; ours, by way of little acts of kindness, mingled by way of wholesome tonic with wise advice; these things made him not a physician, but a friend ... A batch of heavy cases involving all-night sittings made him a dangerously easy prey to the illnesses it was his life's work to combat.'

A further appreciation was added by Dr McAldowie, a fellow medical officer at the Red Cross Hospital at Leckhampton Court, where Dr Lloyd Davies had served from 1915 to 1919.

ADVERTISEMENTS

Advertisements became a regular feature after 1918, exploiting the full range of typefaces available at the time. As many as 30 or 40 per issue, they remind us of shops and tradespeople in the village and the Bath Road area (where the distinction between the 'Upper' and 'Lower' sections was stressed) as well as further afield. Most of the businesses have long since vanished but others survived until more recently. In a few cases the premises remain but there has been a change in commercial use. Some local family names also strike a chord.

The names of a few local businesses advertised in the 1920s and '30s may still be recognised. LEIGH JAMES, Family Butcher – now Bath Road Butchers – offered 'Deliveries throughout Leckhampton daily'. C E LEAT in Bath Road was advertised as 'Stationer, newsagent and fancy goods dealer, the leading shop in Leckhampton for stationery and writing materials'. Others were W J COURT, English and foreign fruiterer, SINGLETONS, 'The People's clothiers, outfitters and hosiers'. GILBEY COOLE, Ironmonger of Bath Road – taken over by Newmans which in turn has merged with Bloodworths – began to advertise in the early 1930s ('Judge' hollow-ware and 'Royal Daylight' lamp oil, for example).

From 1918 JOHN CAUDLE & SONS, of 49 Upper Bath Road, advertised boots & shoes, 'Bespoke orders and repairs all done on the premises'. JOHN D BENDALL & SONS (J L Bendall, M.R.S.I., Lond.) offered a wide range of building services, including 'Gas work & bell hanging ... geometrical, mosaic, encaustic, plain & ornamental tile laying'.

SMITH BROS, 'Manufacturers of all kinds of Woodwork', from an address in Albion Street offered 'wash up tubs, either square or round, drinking troughs for stables or road use, shepherds' houses, fixtures or on wheels, wireless poles and aerials supplied and erected complete'. Their bungalows and rustic summer houses can be seen on the whole page advertisement reproduced overleaf.

The village in former years could evidently support a number of businesses. E FEATHERSTONE, Coal and Timber Merchant, of Tregantle, Church Road, had a wharf at Leckhampton Station; Leckhampton Quarries, with its registered office at the wharf in Leckhampton Road, advertised in 1922 (four years before it finally ceased working); H BECK (later A R NORMAN), Monumental Sculptor, had both works and residence at Cleobury, Old Bath Road; and CHICK & BRIDGES (later A R CHICK), Motor Engineers of Church Road (occupying a workshop which remained in business until recently), boasted 'Open and Closed Cars for Hire, Distance No Object'; and JOHN BARRETT, of Southwold Gardens, Leckhampton Road, offered fresh fruit, flowers and vegetables – prompt deliveries anywhere – and care of graves at Leckhampton churchyard.

SUMMER HOUSES, made in sections and easily erected.

Garden Frames, Greenhouses and Repairs.

PIG COTS, GARDEN GATES. FENCING, BUNGALOWS AND ALL PORTABLE BUILDINGS,

WASH UP TUBS, either square or round, any size.

DRINKING TROUGHS for stables or road use.

PAY BOXES for sports, race meetings, fetes, etc.

SHEPHERDS' HOUSES, fixtures or on wheels.

BUNGALOWS, special designs, and with any fitments.

PACKING CASES, for English or Foreign transit.

CARPENTERS' BENCHES, any size or thickness.

CATTLE FEEDERS, iron or wood with or without roof.

SHEEP TROUGHS, open or covered in any wood or iron.

PIG TROUGHS, made in deal, elm, oak or other wood.

BOOK SHELVES, in deal, oak, walnut and mahogany.

COAL and CINDER BOXES, plain or with rockers.

HAND TRUCKS for all trades, or repairs at lowest prices.

GREENHOUSE STAGING, plain or painted, any dimensions.

Wireless Poles and Aerials Supplied and Erected complete

SMITH BROS.

Manufacturers of all kinds of Woodwork,

Offices and Saw Mills :

Phone 2788 **ALBION STREET, Cheltenham.** Phone 2788

An advertisement from 1933

Some advertisements from the 1920s and 1930s

The 'Pop-in' late-opening grocery in Hall Road, which a few years ago was converted back into an ordinary dwelling, was the PROSPECT SUPPLY STORES in the 1920s and 30s. (Prospect Cottage in Moorend Road today reminds us of the former name of that corner of the village – 'Prospect Place'.) It was a grocery, provision merchant's and off-licence, offering a wide range of beers and ciders, including the now unfamiliar Whiley's and Henley's ciders – 'A Trial Solicited. Delivery to all parts daily'.

Some of the grander household names from Cheltenham must have thought it worthwhile to advertise in the magazine. We regularly see SHIRER & HADDON (later Shirer & Lance's) 'General Drapers, Costumiers and Ladies' Outfitters', and DALE, FORTY, of The Promenade, for pianos and radio. Advertisements for CAVENDISH HOUSE began to appear after the Second World War. By 1929, THE FAMOUS was advertising British-made clothing for men and boys, and soon after that the CHELTENHAM & GLOUCESTER Building Society began to feature, illustrating its advertisement with a neatly fenced semi-detached house of the period.

The goods and services offered reflect the social and other conditions of the time. After the First World War, BALLINGER BROS and WILLIAMS had set up as cabinet makers, upholsterers and picture framers, 'Practical Men, Demobolised' (*sic*), and H HARPER '(Bluthner, Wigmore Street, London) Co-Sergt-Maj discharged through wounds' sought work as a piano-tuner in addition to selling gramophones, records, pianos and music. W SHARPE & SONS, of Colonnade House, Cheltenham, were 'Military Bootmakers', while J JONES, a 'Practical boot maker' of Edward Terrace, Norwood Road, stressed that he was 'close to trams'. JAMES CYPHER & SONS recommended the Queens Road Nursery as being 'near the Midland Station'. In 1920 ERNEST J TUCKER, of Upper Bath Road, was a 'Photographic Artist – please don't read this and then forget it'! FARRAR'S offered 'fascinating fuels'. JOYNER & SON of 31 Suffolk Parade were brush manufacturers, 'all kinds made to order (or refilled) on the shortest notice'. GILCHRIST of 19 & 20 Great Norwood Street would overhaul cycles, while WHEWAY of 2 & 3 Suffolk Road and STRANGER'S of Montpellier dealt in baby carriages.

In 1923 advertisements by Spirella Corsets, with punctuation looser than their undergarments, proclaimed

Ladies' waited on at their own homes
Resident Corsetierè. (*sic*)

In 1928 F & A MARCH of 373 High Street provided typewriting and duplicating services as well as teaching typewriting and speedwriting. In 1930 another shop offered 'Electrolux for hire'. In 1936 'Leckhampton Charging Station' would supply radios, 'both portable and self-contained'. A dentist, William E Wincott, claimed to provide 'Painless Dentistry' at 3 Pittville Street: 'Painless extractions before 10 a.m., 1 shilling'.

SPECIAL FEATURES

'Botanical Notes for the Working Man'

Robert Cary Barnard (grandfather of the late Major Tom Barnard) was an eager and prolific contributor to the magazines. He wrote a number of 'Botanical Notes for the Working Man' which were printed during 1899. These are full of sharp observation and interesting digressions. He wrote of the germination of seeds and the appearance of the first flowers: 'So far as my observation goes, these are always what are called *Male Flowers*. They will not produce fruit any more than the cock in the poultry yard or the drone in the hive will produce eggs that are destined to grow into chickens and bees.' He also anticipates the current vogue for cocoa fibre as a garden mulch.

Writing of the Eucalyptus tree, he adds: 'Remembering that Australia had practically been known to us for not more than 100 years, may we not look upon it as an area specially reserved during all the bygone ages for the use of the Anglo-Saxon race, and shall we not all heartily rejoice in the Australians' favourite motto – 'Advance Australia!'.

R C Barnard was receptive to new ideas too. Discussing the blackberry, he wrote: 'Among the numerous American varieties is one called the *Logan-berry* which seems likely to be a good thing. I had some really good berries of it sent to me last year: they were red, larger than any blackberry or raspberry I had ever seen, and the flavour I thought as good as could be expected after a journey through parcel-post ... It was raised by Judge Logan of California in, 1882 and is a cross between the dewberry (*Rubus vitifolius*) and a Red Antwerp raspberry.'

Local History

The chapters of R C Barnard's book *Records of Leckhampton* were originally serialised in the Parish Magazines for 1897. This book was a survey of the history of the parish from the Anglo-Saxon period to the beginning of the 19th century, and it remains the most detailed and comprehensive study of the subject so far published.

In 1899 some papers were printed on 'Our Parish Church' by Henry Middleton, the son of the architect John Middleton who had been responsible for the church's enlargement in 1866-68. Also an architect, he would have been well informed on the earlier state of the building. I have already taken account of some of this article when writing *The History of Leckhampton Church*, but some interesting facts and observations are worth repeating here.

Middleton confirms that before the enlargement the south aisle was separated from the nave by a 'low Norman arcade of three arches' of which a half-column remains at the east end, showing that the original Norman church also had a south aisle. He reminds us that the effigies of Sir John and Lady Giffard, now at the back of the church, used to lie near the altar of the south aisle.

Concerning the churchyard, he refers to a number of stone coffin lids, which he dates to the 14th century (ie roughly contemporary with Sir John Giffard), while a recumbent effigy of a priest in the churchyard outside was 'suffering from the effects of the weather and it would be well if it could be replaced in the church under shelter'. The effigy now rests inside the church near the font, but it was not until 1907 that, according to Canon Henry Proctor, 'thirteen ancient and interesting tombstones which were lying in different parts of the churchyard, covered with moss ... [were] placed together on either side of the entrance porch and the four recumbent figures among them railed in'.

In 1925 Captain John Trye contributed some articles on 'The Manors of Leckhampton'. Supposing that it might be news to some that there were originally *two* manors in Leckhampton, he reproduced the Roll of a Court session for the 'second' manor, held in 1691 under the Lordship of Edward Nourse. He observed that the 1746 Leckhampton Court Estate map showed in a field behind the Rectory 'Mr Nourse's farm house ... [whose] remains will no doubt be recollected by some of the older inhabitants of the parish'. (The remaining traces of this building were covered by soil in the 1980s. More recently Terry Moore-Scott has identified a third manorial estate – see Leckhampton LHS *Research Bulletin* No 4.)

In 1929 an article by Captain Trye was printed concerning the life of Colonel Henry Norwood. It describes Henry Norwood's hazardous voyage to Virginia, during which food ran so short that a well grown rat was sold for 16 shillings, and when Norwood was marooned on an island five of his party died of cold and starvation 'and the survivors turned their carcases into food'. (The full account is given in the *Transactions of the Bristol & Gloucestershire Archaeological Society* (*TBGAS*), Vol XLVII.)

Leckhampton, alias 'Leckington'

We are reminded more than once of a historic alternative name for the village – 'Leckington' or 'Lackington'. This name will still have been familiar to many inhabitants. For example, in 1922 the Reverend F R Standfast described the pantomime (*Rumpelstiltskin*) as having 'gladdened the hearts of the folks of 'LACKINGTON', and he also urged parishioners not to be 'lacking in love for God and gratitude to our pious forefathers; Leckhampton need not be 'LACKING-TON' in these things'. Then in 1932, Mr Ernest Parsons, on giving up the Headmastership of Leckhampton School, chose 'Leckington' as the name of his new house in Kingston-on-Thames.

The Excavation of the Moat

In 1933 there was a thorough excavation of the Moat, opposite the church, led by Major J G N Clift. Archdeacon Sears adds a contemporary comment:

> 'The dry summer gave an opportunity for excavation of the Moat
> – the foundations of the old bridge were laid bare, the origin of
> which caused much difference of opinion amongst antiquaries –
> one view was that the stones, and presumably the original bridge,
> dated back to Norman times – another was that the date could not
> be placed earlier than the 14th century. The probability is that
> there was in very early days a house on the island formed by the
> Moat, and that when Leckhampton Court was built the 'Moat
> House' was pulled down and such materials as were available
> were used in the construction of the Court.'

'The Bridal of Alice Bredone'

The Bridal of Alice Bredone, a so-called legend of Leckhampton Church, was serialised in 1929. It is a fanciful and melodramatic yarn, with a sinister cowled monk (the villain in disguise) coming between Alice Bredone and her betrothed Sir John Gifford as the maid expires at the very wedding altar, and 'bridal and burial formed but the same day's ceremony'! It appears far removed from any historical fact, and its mock-medieval style is highly contrived. It was reprinted from *The Cheltenham Album*, published by H Davies in 1831.

The Russian Police

An article on the Russian Police, which appeared in June 1888, includes a description of the Secret Police which could have applied equally well to the Soviet KGB. From its attentions 'no one, not even a British resident, is absolutely secure ... he will find his movements impeded and questioned at every turn, and will probably end by being turned out of the place if he wishes to remain in, or kept there if he particularly desires to go!' The writer was Frederick Whishaw, of The Grotto, Moorend Road, who wrote adventure books set in Russia, where he had been born..

Red Cross Voluntary Aid Detachment at Leckhampton Court

Because no magazines are available for the early years of the First World War, the only mention of the Red Cross Hospital at Leckhampton Court was in August 1918, when the Commandant sent her thanks to those who helped to make a fundraising fête a success.

OMISSIONS

There is no mention of the sale of the Leckhampton Court estate in 1894, even though it was 'the most important event to have occurred in the village in modern times' (*Leckhampton 1894*, ed Bruce Stait). The dispute over access to the hill at the turn of the century evidently also passed without comment. On the other hand, silence on this controversial subject may have been the only discrete course of action, since Henry John Dale, who had bought the quarries when the Leckhampton estate was sold in 1894, and who later took the unpopular action of fencing off the hill, was a churchwarden, while Major Barnard and family, G B Witts and other church people had been offended by Dale's action and actively supported the protest of the 'Leckhampton Stalwarts'.

Some advertisements from the 1920s and 1930s

More advertisements from the 1920s and 1930s

Chapter Two
THE PARISH HALL

The architect H A Prothero's impression of the Parish Hall

FUNDRAISING AND BUILDING

The building of the Parish Hall was perhaps the single most important factor in cementing the sense of village identity at the turn of the century. The private houses of the gentry were no longer suitable or large enough to accommodate the increasing numbers of people eager to meet together, and the old school (later used as the dining hall), though more centrally located, was also inadequate as a venue. The creation of the Parish Hall was due very largely to the efforts of the Reverend Clifford Aston, who came to the parish in 1895. He saw that the hall would answer a need and that once it was built it would in turn provide further opportunities for communal entertainment, recreation and self-improvement.

The following quotations from Clifford Aston's reports in the Parish Magazines give us something of the flavour of his crusade, for which we have every reason to be grateful today. The episode began in November 1895, when a fundraising concert was held in the schoolroom itself:

'It was unfortunate that the room was not capacious enough to hold all who wished to be present. But you will kindly take this as a strong and pressing argument for the erection, as soon as possible, of a Parish Hall, which, in these days, is positively essential to progressive church work. I have received a donation of £50 for this purpose, and have opened a fund in the Post Office Savings Bank. £300 will, I believe, suffice to supply such a room as we want and ... what a privilege is theirs, who have it in their power to give a good round sum to so helpful a work!'

By January a site had been earmarked and Henry Prothero had designed the building. (The architect's impression of the building, with the Devil's Chimney imaginatively looming behind, is reproduced on the previous page.)

In November 1896 a grand bazaar was held over three days at the Montpellier Rotunda in aid of the project. Sir John Dorington (the then MP for Cirencester) was singled out for his 'witty speech into the Phonograph' – an invention which would clearly have been a great novelty to all present. From the proceeds the first instalment of £200 was paid to Collins and Godfrey, the builders.

It was found necessary to acquire additional land, which was paid for by 'the same good friend [a lady] who gave the original piece'. Early in 1897 a further extension of land was purchased by G B Witts to provide 20 feet more frontage and 12 feet more depth, offering 'space for a carriage to sweep up to the door'.

Less than 18 months elapsed between the design of the building to its completion, and it was on 26th April 1897 that the first event was held in the new hall, a grand concert in aid of the National School. Clifford Aston's original guess of £300 for the total cost of the hall proved very conservative, however. The final bill for what was regarded as one of the permanent memorials of the Queen's reign came to over five times that amount and was not paid off until 1904.

BENEFACTORS

Quite apart from making gifts of money, individual benefactors were responsible for certain specific items. The donor of the clock, at first coyly described as 'a lady well known to most of us', later proved to be Mrs Margaret Riddle, the widow of the first Vicar of St Philip and St James's.

In March 1901 Miss Swift – 'so generous and practical a helper to the parish, not once or twice!' – was identified by Clifford Aston as having paid for the gates. 'The cross keys that crown them let there be no mistake as to whom the building belongs.' (He was of course referring to St Peter's Church: the ownership was vested in the Gloucestershire Diocesan Trust, and the Committee of Managers consisted of the Rector, the two Churchwardens and four male communicants. This came to an end in 1986 and as a consequence the building is now referred to as the *Village* Hall.)

Mrs Meredith gave a clock for the inside and 4 dozen teacups and saucers of Meissner ware, to supplement the 4 dozen Jubilee cups and saucers which had already been provided. Clifford Aston also appealed for a harmonium, coal scuttles and fire irons.

THE CLOCK

Clifford Aston was pleased to report that the Queen's Day also saw the new clock going on the outside of the building – 'a great acquisition for the Parish'. The cost of winding up the clock was included in the charges for using the hall. (After another appeal one hundred years later, the clock has been replaced by a new one, which will not need winding.)

LATER DEVELOPMENTS

Improvements were gradually introduced, with the result that the building is still very much in demand for a variety of uses. The first significant change was mooted in 1907, when it was proposed to open the hall for the use of the whole parish for badminton and ping pong. This became possible in 1911, when the platform was rearranged, the fixed portion being made narrower to allow a full-sized badminton court on the floor of the hall.

In 1926 electric light was installed, and in 1929 the heating arrangements were improved. It was also observed that the managers needed to safeguard themselves against infringements of copyright music at entertainments. An additional charge of two shillings was therefore levied in all cases where the entertainment included music, to defray this 'somewhat heavy annual cost'.

MEMORIAL TO THE REVEREND CLIFFORD ASTON

It is fitting that the brass plaque which was eventually placed in the hall – a fine one, surrounded by garlands of leaves, rosebuds and rosettes in yellow and dark green, above the mantelshelf of the fireplace – was a memorial to Clifford Aston himself, following his untimely death. The inscription reads:

THIS TABLET PLACED HERE BY FRIENDS
AND PARISHIONERS IS A TOKEN OF THEIR
LOVE AND ESTEEM FOR THE
REV W CLIFFORD ASTON MA
FOR 8½ YEARS CURATE-IN-CHARGE OF
ST PETER'S PARISH CHURCH, LECKHAMPTON.
HE DIED FEBRUARY 13TH. 1904
BUILT MAINLY THROUGH HIS ENERGY AND EFFORTS
THIS HALL WAS COMPLETED IN THE 60TH YEAR
OF THE REIGN OF H M QUEEN VICTORIA
AUGUST 1905

Chapter Three
CLUBS, SOCIETIES AND SPORT

Clifford Aston was responsible at the turn of the century for encouraging the creation and growth of many organisations in the parish, some of which are described below. A few charitable groups already existed, of course, but new clubs and societies were set up, designed to improve their members' spiritual well-being and their practical skills, and also if possible to be of benefit to the rest of the community. Members of the local well-to-do families helped in the running.

THE PARISH LIBRARY

A Parish Library had evidently existed in one form or another before 1895, in which year Miss Sarah Trye and Mrs Jane Meredith (daughters of the previous Rector, C B Trye) volunteered to re-establish it with 'a really good collection of books, and up-to-date – Ballantine and Kingston, and Louis Stevenson and G A Henty, and Miss Holt and *Uncle Tom's Cabin*'. Clifford Aston hoped to 'kill out the mischievous effects of the "Penny Dreadful" and other such stuff as poisons the minds of our young people'. The Library opened with 200 volumes and issued nearly 70 books on its first day. A 7-year old wanting to take home a copy of the *Strand Magazine* was cited as evidence of the eager thirst for knowledge of the younger generation. By 1897 the number of volumes had increased to over 600. Books were issued free, but fines were levied.

The initial enthusiasm was evidently not maintained, however. A sad note from Mrs Meredith in 1901 stated that she had received no further subscriptions or donations and only three gifts of books. This was followed some months later by an announcement that the Library would be relaunched with a great many fresh books. Acknowledgements were made to Mr Walker (a Churchwarden) and Miss Swift (for the third time) and Mrs Nathaniel Smith.

After an interruption for the First World War, the Parish Library was again reopened in 1920, with advice from Mr Sidney Harrison, the Cheltenham Town Librarian. The stock of books was over 1000 and covered a wide range of subjects. In its first year the membership was 250 and on average 100 books were issued each week, at a charge of one penny per book. The opening hours were 3 – 5.30 p.m. for adults, 4 – 4.45 p.m. for children. The library was run by Miss Gladys Duckworth and Miss S Ivelaw-Chapman, but when the latter left to take up social work in Birmingham in 1923, her sister Miss Eileen took over. (Shortly before her hundredth birthday Miss Eileen told me that the library was held in the kitchen of the Parish Hall and that it was open one day a week, when the Mothers' Union met.) By 1928 the library's weekly session was held in the school, its stock had risen to 1200 books and there were about 150 regular borrowers, many of whom were children. It was described as 'the only school library in Gloucestershire'.

This Parish Library was of course unconnected with the Free Reading Rooms, opened to the general public in 1894, which were housed in the Local Board Room in Moorend Road. (This building now serves as an electricity substation.) In 1905 there was an announcement that the Rooms, which were open every day from 3 p.m. to 9.30 p.m., were well supplied with daily and weekly illustrated papers and magazines. It further stated that books from the Public Library could be exchanged there and that the beginnings of a permanent library had been made. However, it was not until 1st April 1935 that the inhabitants of Leckhampton were allowed free use of Cheltenham Public Library, according to a letter addressed to the Rector by the Town Librarian, which was quoted in the magazine.

PRACTICAL RECREATION CLASSES

A Girls' Recreation Class was started under Miss Trye and Mrs Meredith. This 'promised to be of great practical benefit for their future careers. There is to be a little house in miniature, in which the girls will learn household work of all kinds (after the German method of training)'. This is a reminder that many of the village girls would have expected to go into domestic service. In the same way, we read that at Sunday afternoon Bible Classes 'any young girls and servants would be made welcome'.

In 1897 it had been hoped to arrange technical instruction classes in cookery, home nursing and dressmaking for the girls, and carpentry, gardening, and first aid for the lads and young men. These did not come about, however, as the Cheltenham Committee had been unable to obtain adequate funds from the County Council. On a more modest scale, a course of ten lessons in Cottage Cookery was advertised the following

January, to be held in the Parish Hall. The Boys' Recreation Class, led by the Misses Riley, produced fretwork and paintings for sale. Mrs Meredith donated two pairs of brass candlesticks, as 'the boys required a nearer light for their woodcarving'. In 1901 Will Townsend won the prize for Deep Wood Carving, and in 1903 Miss Vavasour took 24 different pieces of woodcarving to an art exhibition in Gloucester. She and Miss Witts (her half-sister) were duly praised for their able tuition.

BOYS' ORGANISATIONS

The Church Lads' Brigade and Scouting

The fortunes of the Church Lads' Brigade and the evolution of the new Scout Movement are described in the early magazines. In 1901 a company of the Church Lads' Brigade was started under the captaincy of Mr Robert Marshall with assistance from Mr Louis Sharpe, and by 1903 it had 36 members. The company met in the Parish Hall; it was separate from the St Philip and St James's company, which met in the old school at the bottom of Leckhampton Road.

Shooting was an important pursuit for the boys, and the accounts showed the purchase of carbines, with rack, padlock and keys. They also bought two bugles and side drums, which provoked the observation that 'the buglers and drummers practise their respective parts about our fields and roads; this we hope to check'. All their training will have been necessary to ensure a smart turnout when they formed part of the bodyguard for Field Marshal Lord Roberts during his visit to Cheltenham in 1904. On a lighter note, in 1909 they put on a pantomime, *The Pied Piper*, for which the Girls' Club also joined in, directed by Lieutenant L W Barnard. (His leadership of the Camberwell CLB is described in Chapter 5.)

In September 1909 (the year after *Scouting for Boys* had been first published) it was announced that the Church Lads' Brigade would incorporate 'scouting', so as not to fall behind in this new development. The local patrol of the 'ICSP' (Incorporated Church Scout Patrols, later known simply as the Church Scouts) was seen as forming a sort of cadet corps to the Church Lads' Brigade. By 1910 some twenty boys aged 11 – 14 had joined, at first under Sergeant Jenkins, while ten Brigade members passed on to the Territorial Army.

On Easter Monday 1910 the Scouts, assisted by seven members of the Church Lads' Brigade, had a despatch-running competition. Two boys reached the Rectory without being caught, one having started from the Badgeworth turning on the Shurdington Road, and the other from Lansdown Castle. On Whit Monday there was a Grand Review of all the companies of CLB and ICSP in the diocese, held by invitation of Mr Vassar-Smith in Charlton Park, at which the Bishop, the Mayor of Cheltenham and possibly Lord St Aldwyn were expected to be present. On Boxing Day there was a Grand Field Day at Painswick, with bands drawn from Painswick, Gloucester and Nailsworth. The day began with a church service to admit new members, followed by some skirmishing, then tea.

The magazines made no further mention of the Scouts or the Church Lads' Brigade, except in 1934, when it was evident that the Scouts at least were still flourishing. In that year the Leckhampton Troop of Baden Powell Scouts moved into their new headquarters, 'a commodious hut ... above Undercliffe Terrace', on a site provided by Councillor Alfred Bendall. Mrs Trye (of 'The Grotto', wife of Captain John Trye) performed the opening ceremony on 16th April. The Scoutmaster was Mr H Gurney, of 'Athlone,' Mead Road. (The late Arthur Bendall, Alfred's nephew, told me that this wooden hut was dismantled and moved to family-owned land at the end of Pilford Avenue in 1947. The present Scout HQ, beside the old caravan factory, did not come into use until after the Second World War.)

The Lads' Club

Other provision for the boys of the parish after the First World War seems to have been on less military lines. In the 1920s a Lads' Club was formed, for boys of 16 – 20 years. It met twice weekly. Tuesdays were 'quiet evenings' devoted to reading and sit-down games such as draughts and chess. Ping-pong, bagatelle, darts, quoits and skittles were allowed only on Thursdays.

The title of the club was soon changed to the Young Men's Club, and in 1926 it held a dance at which many of the girls from the Girls' Club were present. There was music from a jazz band, 'with which most of those present were well content'. The young men also held debates and even a mock trial, a shocking murder case, to be tried at the next 'Leckhampton Assizes'. Maybe this was prompted by some of the authors whom they voted their favourites in 1927: Edgar Wallace, Sapper, Rider Haggard, Conan Doyle, H G Wells, Dumas, Raphael

Sabatini, Sax Rohmer, Philip Oppenheim, Roland Pertwee, Zane Grey, Jeffrey Farnol and William le Queux.

GIRLS' ORGANISATIONS

The Girls' Friendly Society

A branch of the Girls' Friendly Society was in existence at the beginning of the 20th century. One of its events recorded in 1906 (perhaps not entirely typical) consisted of tea in the Parish Hall, a service in church with an address by Canon Proctor on the danger of a frivolous and irreverent spirit, a return to the Parish Hall for an 'earnest' address with lantern slides by Miss Townsend on the work of the GFS in India, and finally entertainment (not *too* frivolous, one hopes!) 'which carried on the assembly in a very happy mood to quite a late hour'.

The Girls' Friendly Society held a hockey dance in 1927 to raise funds for the Hockey Club. The girls cannot have been particularly affluent themselves, as in the following year the GFS Candidates' Class put in a plea for 'scraps and stout brown paper for scrap books'. By 1929, together with the Girls' Club they were hoping to establish a small tennis club, and invited gifts of old tennis rackets and balls.

The branch occasionally arranged talks, for example in 1934 Mrs Captain John Trye's wife Betty gave them a 'most interesting and amusing account of her European trip in the Riley Car Rally'.

The range of the girls' accomplishments is indicated by the assortment of subjects for which awards were made to candidates and members in 1935. As well as written GFS knowledge and the keeping of the branch log book (possibly in competition with the St Philip and St James's branch), the headings included needlework (team and individual), cooking, piano, country dancing, original dance in costume, choir, recitation, march, drama (advanced), poetry, slipper making, laundry, photography, general knowledge, penmanship, sleeveless overall, painted wood, papier mâché, and water colour painting.

The Girls' Drill Club

In January 1909 a physical drill class was started for girls. Fourteen girls gave a public display the following year in the use of dumb-bells, bat-bell drill (*sic*), free movement, skipping and jumping, ending up with a fairy-light march.

The club finished its 1922 season by giving a display in the Parish Hall. The smallest member of the club presented Miss Gerda Elwes (herself aged only 11), who had come to confer the badges, with a bouquet, tied with the club colour of red. Twenty-six girls in all, looking very smart in their white blouses, blue slips and red belts, performed Swedish drill and mass exercises with Indian clubs, dumb bells and wands. Eight of them came skipping in for country dances and dances round a maypole. Captain John Trye, who presided over the occasion, thanked the girls and said that great credit was due to their leader, Miss Fordham, and to show their appreciation the girls presented her with an ivory-bound hymn and prayer book.

The Girls' Club

A separate Girls' Club also existed, as we have already seen, with a more sociable purpose. In 1919 Lady Winterbotham presented badges at the Girls' Club entertainment (for which tickets were available only in advance, not at the door). In 1926 the club was retitled 'St Peter's Ladies' Club', to conform with the 'Young Men's Club' – see above.

The Girl Guides

As for the Girl Guides, in April 1932 it was announced that two ladies had offered to inaugurate a troop in the parish, and that the Church Council would provide financial help from funds in the Free Will Offering Fund. Nothing further was said on the subject in the magazines of the time, though a troop was started in due course.

THE CHURCH OF ENGLAND MEN'S SOCIETY

The menfolk of the parish had been in the habit of holding informal social evenings 'over a pipe and a cup of coffee', including 'smoking concerts' in the Parish Hall. In the November of 1901 they formed themselves into a branch of the Church of England Men's Society, after one was said to have been in existence in the neighbouring parish of St Philip and St James's for some years. The branch started enthusiastically, with 40 members. The subscription was two pence a week, and the lower age limit was 16. The members were loaned a billiard table and a 'shuvette table, on which a fascinating game is played by as many as eight at a time'. (A surviving example of this game is to be seen at Dunham Massey House in Cheshire.) The men also made good use of a bagatelle board, presented to the Parish Hall by Miss Webster of Newholme.

By 1906 the men enjoyed the use of 'premises granted to them on very easy terms' by Captain Cecil Elwes. Billiards was provided inside and a shooting range outside. (The actual building in Church Road, now known as 'Old Farthings', had been a club house for workers on the Leckhampton estate.)

These pipe-smoking marksmen and billiard players, though calling themselves members of the CEMS, cannot have been affiliated to the national organisation, for in 1907 a fully constituted branch was started, with 32 members. The only absolute condition of membership was daily prayer and work for Christ. Meetings were held fortnightly on Sunday afternoons, services in church alternating with discussions in the Parish Hall. Guests were invited; in July 1907 eleven members of the Gloucester Gordon League Cycling Club were present. Not all events were for men only; for one of the social evenings members were asked to 'bring wives (or next best) and their music and accomplishments' (!).

By 1909, enthusiasm had waned, but to raise funds their 'friends at the Court' (ie members of the Elwes family) gave 'two magnificent entertainments' and the men themselves organised contributions of their own, for example a 'capital programme of music at a smoking concert'. By the following year the Leckhampton group was one of ten branches in Cheltenham affiliated to the Diocesan Union, itself embracing 65 branches. (A Diocesan Gathering of the CEMS held at Coleford the previous summer is described in Chapter 4.)

Inevitably, the Men's Society was dormant during the First World War, though a Branch Secretary (Mr C F Hall, of Treelands) was still listed. There are few other references to its activities during the ensuing years. One delegate from the parish was among the 700 who attended the CEMS Conference in Bristol in 1925. There is no entry for a Branch Secretary after 1935, and it must be surmised that interest had waned to such an extent that the branch ceased to meet. Further research may reveal otherwise, but the likelihood is that the Leckhampton Branch was moribund until its revival well after the end of the Second World War, in March 1984. This branch in turn survived the eventual demise of the CEMS as a national organisation as the Leckhampton Men's Society, affiliated to the Gloucester Diocesan Men's Society until it too folded in 1998.

THE MOTHERS' MEETING AND MOTHERS' UNION

The Leckhampton branch of the Mothers' Union is known to have been founded in 1913, but the ladies of the parish had been getting together in a less formal way since as early as 1891, when there was a report of the 'Mothers' Meetings' held that year. (This just precedes the formation of the Diocesan MU in November of that year, though the 'Mothers' Union' title was used loosely before that.) The report was signed by Mrs Dale, of Daisy Bank House, the wife of Henry John Dale (of Dale, Forty, the music dealers, and owner of the Leckhampton Quarries).

'Through the kindness of a few friends the above meetings were begun,' wrote Mrs Dale 'and are increasingly appreciated by the members.' A financial statement lists the names of the thirteen other members. Their addresses give us some idea of their standing: Firs Brake, Hill House, Gwynfa, Ashmeade, Undercliff, Southfield and Wychbury. Expenditure consisted mainly of the 'drapery account' (£12-17s-5½d), while 15s-8d had gone on 'firing and attendant'.

The ladies met as a rule on Monday afternoons at the Parish Hall or in the schoolroom. On at least one occasion their husbands were also invited for tea and a social, when there were speeches and solos and Mrs Dale was presented with a 'handsome inkstand and a morocco blotter'. Other regular social events were the annual outings, some of which are described in Chapter 4.

The Mothers' Meeting sponsored further good work, such as:

• A Maternity Society, whose cases would be attended to by Dr Pruen, of Suffolk Place

• A Blanket Club (designed to help the poorer residents of the Parish, in an age before organised social security); during 1898 it issued 17 blankets. The terms of payment were involved but not unduly demanding: three half-crowns over a period of three years, after which the blankets became the property of the lessee. There was a rebate if blankets were returned, washed, earlier than that.

• A branch of the Women's Help Society (motto 'Onward and Upward'), with Miss Vavasour as Secretary. No subscription was required. In 1901 some 50-60 people attended a meeting of the Society in the Parish Hall. (A similar organisation also existed in those days for men.)

- A Women's Work Association, which in 1902 subscribed to a 'beautifully wrought white altar cloth'

- A Mothers' Sewing Class

There was also a Ladies' Knitting Guild, which was formed in 1900 to prepare knitted and woollen articles of clothing for the soldiers fighting in the Boer War. There were two groups, subtly divided according to whether they contributed money or clothing, or whether they simply did some knitting. 'Class A' paid a subscription of one shilling and contributed one article, while 'Class B' received the wool and returned completed articles. The Parish Magazine for March 1900 lists 9 pairs of socks, 82 balaclava helmets, 12 mittens and cuffs, 5 belts and 21 scarves. (Three young men from the parish had volunteered for service in South Africa – see Chapter 5.)

Because of a gap in the run of surviving Parish Magazines, we do not read about the Mothers' Union branch proper until 1918, when Mrs Duckworth, of Rosenhoe, is listed as the Secretary. In 1920 it was felt to be time to get the Mothers' Union on its feet again after the war. 'We want specially all the young wives and mothers, of whom there are a great number, swept into it ... also cousins and aunts.'

The meetings eventually settled into a routine pattern. One unusual activity in the 1930s, however, was the organisation of Bandage Winding Parties in the Parish Hall in aid of missionary hospitals overseas. They made up such items as stocking vests, poultice bags, and knitted caps for lepers. In 1935 428 roller bandages, 44 T-bandages, 24 theatre cloths, 3 draw sheets and 65 towelling squares were sent off to the Dublin University Mission in India. In 1937 71 people came to help. They began at 2.30 p.m. and had to stop earlier than they wished, to attend an 8 p.m. service in church. This time they used 543¾ yards of material, making up 978 bandages of various kinds, Terry squares and towels.

OTHER ORGANISATIONS

The Parish Club

In 1919 a Parish Club was formed 'for recreation and instruction, cinema films, lectures, boxing, gymnastics, dancing, singing or amateur dramatic work'. It was open to all parishioners, and the committee included 'three members of the Baptist connection including one lady'. Presumably with the building of a club house in mind, there was a proposal to purchase a plot of land occupied as a garden by Mr Townsend, but this was vetoed.

The Young Crusaders

This band of youngsters was formed in December 1895, with 24 members, who had shown 'some really good talent in the way of recitation', demonstrated at an entertainment put on in a packed schoolroom. They were led by the Misses Sharpe, but one sister's 'devotion to art' and the marriage of the other, Miss Alice Louise, led to their departure in 1898. In 1901, the Secretary and Superintendent of the Young Crusaders Band of Hope was Miss Lloyd Davies.

Temperance Movement

In September 1909 the Temperance Forward Movement visited Leckhampton. It was commented that 'only some 600,000 take any avowed part in this most important department of the church's work'. Fifteen people attended a talk at the Parish Hall – 'and not one of them a teetotaller!'

SPORTS CLUBS

Clifford Aston must have been keen on sport (a 'Muscular Christian'?), to judge from a remark he made in 1900, when the news of the relief of Mafeking had just come through, that he himself had once fought against Major-General Baden-Powell – in the annual football match of Westminster versus Charterhouse – but lost. He also mentioned watching the cricket at Gloucester together with his son.

Local worthies were keen to ensure the physical wellbeing of the local youth. In 1897 Mr Edwin Howard of Italia gave a gymnastic apparatus 'to develop the muscle and agility of the youth in the parish', and two years later Mr Hargreaves gave two pairs of boxing gloves for the older boys to practise self-defence.

Cricket

Several local cricket clubs were formed at the turn of the century. In June 1895 the first match of Leckhampton Juniors CC was played against Charlton, in the club colours of chocolate and sky blue. It was hoped to find a more suitable ground than the Rectory orchard.

Leckhampton Cricket Club, 1898
The Reverend Clifford Aston on left and Barnard Thompson with beard

Leckhampton 'A' Football Team, 1920
The Captain (with ball) is B C Enoch

In 1898 the Leckhampton Star Cricket Club played 14 matches during the season. Clifford Aston headed the batting averages – 26 runs in 3 innings. By 1903 there were two elevens, while in 1909 18 boys had asked to be members of a third team. Opposing sides at this time included such names as the Gordon League, the Married Men, British Old Boys, Vulcan Iron Works, the Gas Works, the Police, Steel's XI, Cavendish II, Pilley Chapel (or Pilley Temperance), St James's Institute, Charlton Kings, Bourton Vale, and Colesbourne.

In 1910 B Gregory and W Allen were elected captains of the first and second elevens respectively. The Pearman family held several of the other offices around this time: T Pearman was the retiring captain of the first eleven and M Pearman the new vice-captain, while F Pearman was the vice-captain of the second eleven.

The teams played on a ground in Charlton Lane or 'the top of Pilley', but in 1910 there was talk of combining the cricket and football players in one club, for whom a new pitch had been laid behind the school. In 1931 it had to be pointed out that the Sports Club Field was not a public recreation ground, though exception was made for children of Leckhampton School under supervision. (There was no mention of Burrows Field, which was opened in 1930.)

Football

In 1911 F Harley and C Cambridge were captain and 'sub-captain' of the Club First Team and C Merrett and A Enoch held those offices for the Second Team. Mr G Booy was Secretary. After the war the Club was active again, fielding three teams, 'all high in their leagues'. In 1928 the Club won the Gloucestershire Northern Junior Cup.

The Bendall family gave a strong lead to the Football Club. At a football dinner held in August 1922, attended by about 100 people, Alderman J D Bendall was in the chair and 'some very good songs were sung, including a humorous one by Mr Alfred Bendall introducing the names of various players'.

In 1925 Alfred Bendall was also re-elected President of the Leckhampton Sports Club, which formally recognised Tennis members as having the same powers of self-government as the Cricket and Football sections.

Chapter Four
ENTERTAINMENTS

VILLAGE FÊTES

The chief summer event in the village was the Parish Garden Fête. It usually spanned two days during the working week, offering entertainment and also acting as a means of fundraising. The one held in 1898 is described at some length in the magazine and must have been a memorable occasion.

Mr John Hargreaves made available the whole of the ground floor of the Court. Its quadrangle was turned into an Oriental Bazaar in which 'many pretty and charming ladies dispensed their various wares', while on the terrace there was dancing round the maypole. A Ladies' Bicycle Gymkhana was organised by Colonel Ashburner and Captain Heycock, and admiration was expressed for 'the graceful and clever way they managed their iron steeds in various different feats of skill'.

Rowing boat on Liddington Lake, with probably Mrs Newby beside it in apron

Other outdoor events were held in 'Arthur Pearman's Church Meadow' (the field that lies between the Court and the Church). Messrs Hill & Sons, of Coaley near Dursley, provided a steam roundabout 'and other suchlike fun and merriment'. The lake was also used, and thanks were expressed to 'Mrs Newby of Liddington Lake for the loan of the boat, and to Mr T Callaway for manoeuvring it'. Whether this was simply a rowing boat or one of the steamers that feature in photographs of Liddington Lake (the popular pleasure grounds which flourished at that time beside Leckhampton Station), is impossible to say, but it must have been exciting to see a boat of any sort being carted from there and sailed on the lake at Leckhampton Court.

There was conjuring, ventriloquism, performances by Christy Minstrels and *Tableaux Vivants* in the Old Banqueting Hall, while in the 'Court Theatre' Mr Prothero and his Company of Ladies gave a performance of *The Mousetrap* (but *not* Agatha Christie's). Then the theatre was filled again with people anxious to see 'the far-famed mechanical and automatic Waxworks of Mr and Mrs Jarley' (popular local entertainers of the time – a pseudonym for Mr and Mrs A B Wilson). The report comments that 'judging from the hearty laughter and frequent applause (the stern guardian of the law standing on duty at the door was seen to almost smile) Mr and Mrs Jarley must have been well satisfied with the results of their efforts'.

A museum was set up in the billiard room, mainly devoted to curios collected by Mr Hargreaves in his wanderings abroad. A Chinese photograph, entitled *The Happy Despatch*, 'represented some high functionary in the pleasing occupation of pushing a sword with both hands under his fifth rib, and judging from his expression he is not enjoying himself'. It was explained that for a disgraced official this method of dying was the dignified alternative to execution.

In 1903 the 'Village Fête and Monster Fair' was opened by Lady Carrington (by birth a member of the Elwes family). It included a display of Leckhampton pottery – 'representing a distinctly local industry' (the pottery was in Charlton Lane, near where the Cheshire Home is now). Out of doors there were 'all the attractions of a country fair', including a tent pegging competition, running races, tug-of-war, pig-sticking on ponies, donkey polo, boating on the lake (again), decorated mail carts, and a military band on the lawn and terrace. Stabling was provided at Leckhampton Court stables and at Collum End Farm. Prizes in 1930 included 5 hundredweight of coal, a leg of mutton, cheeses, a duck, rabbits, a Thermos flask, and corn to the value of 5 shillings.

The pattern continued largely unchanged until probably 1935, though by then reduced to one mid-week afternoon, hosted by John Hargreaves's daughter Mrs Muriel Elwes. The Day Schools gave two entertainments, and there were games – bowling for a ham, knocking the hat off, shooting with an air gun, Phrenos (a phrenologist, presumably) and smashing crockery. St Philip and St James's Church also had a stall. Refreshments must have been lavish, since 'for ninepence you could have a good plain tea and for a little more you could "eat your head off".'

Not surprisingly, the sun did not always shine on the events. In 1922 the fête was held in heavy rain, and everything, including chairs and a heavy piano, had to be moved from the grounds of the Court to the Parish Hall. In 1931, though the weather was poor, the profits helped repay part of the £900 which the Diocese had lent towards the building of the Infants' School. In 1933 the fête must have been something of a flop. In addition to weather which 'treated us so cruelly', the event clashed with 'a monster political meeting in the neighbourhood, with all sorts of counter-attractions'. (According to the *Gloucestershire Echo* Winston Churchill came to Churchdown on that date to give a speech on India; the torrential rain was remarked on in that newspaper too.)

FLOWER SHOWS

The Leckhampton Flower Show was 'revived' in 1908. It was held in the grounds of the Court and in later years spread into an adjacent field. It aimed to strike a balance between a 'fair' and a 'show', but the main object was 'to encourage good gardening, good poultry keeping, and the keeping of good horses'. In 1921, as well as horse jumping, driving competitions, side shows and entertainments, there was a programme of athletic sports (governed by the Midland Counties AAA) and amateur boxing matches. A dance was held in the evening, at no extra charge. At the same time as the show about 2,000 Public School Cadets were camped nearby, and their regimental band played in the Court grounds.

Another local event of this kind was the Cottagers' Show, held in the grounds of Fullwood Park, by permission of Mrs Bosanquet, and at which the Town Band would play, according to one of the St Philip and St James's Parish Magazines of 1894. Leckhampton gardeners must have been reluctant to take part, however, since in 1896 Clifford Aston lamented that the previous year there had been scarcely an entry from the village.

EXCURSIONS

Communal outings and parties were greatly looked forward to and much enjoyed. The Rectory Orchard was available for smaller parties, but people were keen to travel further afield as the means of transport improved.

Children's Outings

The magazine of July 1896 recorded several jollifications. For their summer outing the Girls' and Boys' Recreation Classes travelled respectively in a large char-a-banc and a waggonette, via Gloucester Road and Down Hatherley towards 'Wainload's Hill', where they enjoyed cricket and football and boating on the river. The Sunday School children took a drive 'for tea, etc' through Birdlip and Cranham Woods. The cost of hiring brakes was £3-15s-0d, paid for by friends' subscriptions. 'We did not arrive home until after 10 o'clock, which was fine for the infants but must not occur again,' admonished Clifford Aston.

The Day Schools' Fête that year was held at Hill House, home of Mr and Mrs G B Witts. The schoolchildren met at the school at 2 p.m., marched to the church with flags and banners for a 10-minute service, and then went up the hill. They sang 'Hurrah for the Union Jack', had tea in a tent, and were joined by others including the bellringers, who rang a 'touch' on their way in honour of Mr and Mrs Witts. Finally, as we so often read, there was dancing to the Cheltenham Town Band.

In 1901 the Girls' Friendly Society was more adventurous and went first by train from the Midland station to Tewkesbury and then on board the steamer *Jubilee* for a trip up the Severn as far as Kempsey, while on another occasion the choirboys went to Lower Lode, sailing up the river by steamer from Gloucester. The following year the Church Lads' Brigade left Leckhampton by the 10.05 train for Stow, where they took part in a military tattoo and torchlight procession, headed by the Stow Bugle Band.

In 1905 the Sunday School treat was held in Pittville Gardens, on a Tuesday. It was open only to those children who had joined the school before Easter. A party of 131, of whom 118 were scholars, drove from the Parish Hall in brakes. They spent four hours in the gardens, playing games, swinging, racing, boating and having tea. They started back at 7.45 p.m., being delayed for a quarter of an hour by a search for a missing infant, who had evidently made his own way back earlier. The following year (without the infants this time) the children drove to Herbert Villa (now Orchard House) in Charlton Kings, where Mr Horace Edwards allowed them full use of his garden and the fields in which he had fitted up 'many wonderful contrivances for the special amusement of children'.

The visit to Charlton Kings was repeated in 1908, nearly a hundred children travelling this time by train, while members of the King's Messengers and Band of Hope went in the other direction, to Churchdown. The now vanished Leckhampton Station came into its own for excursions of this kind.

In 1922 the venue for the Sunday School was the 'celebrated Denley's Pleasure Grounds' in Bishops Cleeve, with their 'swings, see-saws, chutes, coconut shies' and a 'splendid tea in a spacious new hall'. On returning, a special tram conveyed the excited party from the station to Church Road (all of a quarter of a mile?), where, 'on alighting, three cheers were given for Miss Fulton for arranging such a splendid outing'. In 1925, when the Sunday School went to Withington for its outing, a trip by train was already being described as 'quite an event, in these days of motor cars'. At Withington a former inhabitant of Leckhampton, Mr Beale Brown, found the children unintentionally trespassing on his ground but said that he liked them to be there and brought them honey for their tea.

After the 1939 outing the choirboys commented, perhaps with tongue only slightly in cheek, that

> 'the thoughtful railway company prolonged our pleasure by giving us about an hour on our return journey, which we thoroughly appreciated. It IS great fun to find yourself stopping in a station for half an hour, while friendly engine drivers exchange jokes with you. At any rate, we found it so and wished the journey had taken even longer.'

Men's Society Day Out

In 1909 the Church of England Men's Society held its 4th Annual Diocesan Gathering at Coleford. The magazine account gives an insight into 'a good day out' in less hectic times. On the afternoon of Saturday, 17th July, a small contingent from Leckhampton, using excursion tickets supplied for the occasion, took the train to Lydney Junction, where it was joined by members from other branches. From this point a special train conveyed the men to Coleford, arriving at 3.30 p.m. They then proceeded to 'The Marshes', whose beautiful gardens were thrown open for their use, and where they were welcomed by the Bishop. They dispersed to make the most of the various entertainments, including drives in the neighbourhood, short conducted walks, golf, cricket, tennis, croquet and bowls. Cinderford Brass Band played a varied selection of pieces from 2.15 to 5 o'clock, when all adjourned to the Market Place to be photographed. When that was over, between 400 and 500 men took tea, which was followed by speeches. At 6.30 p.m. a procession headed by the band started for the church, where Evensong was sung at 6.40. The proceedings closed with an organ recital by Ambrose Porter, Assistant Organist at Gloucester Cathedral.

The Mothers' Outing

The first Leckhampton Mothers' Outing for which there is a surviving account was in 1905. Not unusually, it was described as being held 'under damp circumstances'. Two brakes and a pony carriage started from the Parish Hall at 1.30 p.m. First they all drove to Chedworth Roman Villa and 'spent a short time viewing the antiquities, then on to Fosse Bridge Inn, where tea had been arranged. Games filled up the time till the return journey was entered upon.' Similarly in 1907 'the weather interfered a good deal with the entire success of the Mothers' Meeting outing to Lower Wainlode'.

The outing in 1922 was a thoroughly modern one. 'Nearly fifty thrifty British housewives went off char-a-banging' to Worcester, taking in a visit to the Porcelain Works. By 1925 they had graduated to the Blue Taxi Company, for whose drivers they were full of praise, with trips to Clevedon and Weston. Fifty-eight adults and a few children went on the Weston outing in 1926 – quite a marathon, it would appear. The party assembled at the Parish Hall at 7.45, and after prayers by Mrs Standfast a start was made at 8 a.m. They reached their destination at 11.40 a.m. after a brief halt on the Downs for refreshments. They returned home at 9.45 p.m. Other outings took the ladies to Weston and Clevedon, Cheddar, Whipsnade (in 1937) and in 1939 to Weymouth, for which they departed at 7 a.m., for a five-hour journey each way.

HOSPITALITY

The Hargreaves and Elwes families who lived at Leckhampton Court were conscientious in playing their part in parish life. Miss Muriel Hargreaves had evidently had theatrical leanings. In December 1898 dramatic performances were laid on at the Court to provide for the furnishing of the Parish Hall. Miss Hargreaves's Company put on some *Tableaux Vivants* ('living pictures' – a favourite genre of the period, as we shall see), and the Reverend H Evan Noott recited 'The Goblins'. Mr John Hargreaves was also said to have entertained a large party of friends to luncheon and dinner, winding up the day with a dance; the account (reproduced from a local newspaper) discreetly did not hint at the identities of any of the guests.

The coming of age of Miss Sybil Witts was celebrated in the grounds of Hill House in 1901. On Friday June 6th there was a general invitation to the residents of the parish. After the Sunday School children had been entertained to tea, officials and members of the Mothers' Meeting, bellringers, Bible and recreation classes, choir and Church Lads' Brigade sat down to a high tea provided by George's. There followed cricket, swings, tennis and other games until the lanterns and fairy lights were lit. In a marquee 'a series of old country dances was indulged in, to the strains of Mr C James's string band'.

The marriage of Miss Muriel Hargreaves to Captain Cecil Elwes in July 1901 generated much excitement. The Reverend Clifford Aston performed the wedding ceremony at the Guards Chapel, Wellington Barracks. Offering 'hearty good wishes' to the bride and groom, he invited contributions beforehand towards 'a suitable present for one who has lived so long in Leckhampton, and, we hope, will spend many more happy years amongst us'.

These good wishes did not go unacknowledged. In the November, to celebrate their homecoming from their honeymoon, the couple treated 300 of the older inhabitants of the village to a dinner in the School followed by dancing in the Parish Hall.

Five years later, in celebration of their wedding anniversary and the birth of their two children, Captain and Mrs Elwes offered hospitality to the whole parish. At 3 p.m. over 300 sat down in a large marquee which filled the quadrangle at the entrance to the Court. At 5 o'clock nearly as many children sat down to tea, and then at 6.30 p.m. people flocked into the grounds to enjoy cricket and other games, while a band played. Later on there was dancing on the lawn, and finally a grand display of fireworks. Clifford Aston opined that 'very much had been achieved by that one day of friendly comradeship amongst neighbours to strengthen the bonds of unity throughout all classes'.

The goodwill was later reciprocated, when Mr Thompson presented the infant son and daughter with 'some little silver gifts on behalf of the parishioners'. The evening's entertainment included a song containing complimentary allusions to the occasion written by William Pearman.

PARTIES AND PERFORMANCES

Parties

At the Sunday School Christmas Treat in 1892 Miss Hargreaves provided 'part of the cake', a gesture which was not as ungenerous as it might sound, since the cake weighed 43 pounds. Mr Hall provided 7 dozen oranges at three shillings and sixpence. Taken together, these figures suggest that the party was well attended, in keeping with the size of the Sunday Schools at that time. The main entertainment consisted of a magic lantern show.

Mr Dale was in the habit of giving an annual dinner for his quarrymen, followed by entertainment. In 1899 this included a soliloquy from *Richard III* and a passage from *Othello*.

On Twelfth Night 1902, after ringing the church bells, some 45 members of the Ringers' Guild sat down to dinner at the Parish Hall, where they continued with handbell ringing and singing, rounded off by the National Anthem.

Concerts and Pantomimes

The concert programmes were clearly very popular with all ages, though they seem old-fashioned to us today (and certain of the titles would be completely unacceptable). In March 1896 Clifford Aston wrote that 'our friends the "Minstrels", sparkling with wit and merriment, kept us going hard with laughter and applause from 8 to 10.30 p.m.'. The names of those taking part are also of interest, the families from the Court and their friends not being above putting in an appearance, and perhaps even expecting to be asked:

Pianoforte: 'Selections from *The Gondoliers*' – Miss V Hicks-Beach
Song (in character): ''Tis a fine hunting day' – Mr G B Witts

'Twenty-one' – Mrs Clifford Aston
'Temperance Boys and Girls are we' – The Young Crusaders
'The Whistling Coon' – Mr Yeend
Mandolin trio – Misses Muriel Hargreaves, Maitland Reid and Norris
'The Bird and the Rose' – Miss Forbes-Robertson.

Members of the theatrical Forbes-Robertson family cropped up on other occasions, Miss Helen and Miss Ann performing in *Storm in a Teacup* in 1899, for example.

Enthusiastic amateurs wrote and produced their own pantomimes. Leonard Barnard and his sister Christine ('Barnards Unlimited') revived *The Pied Piper* in 1920, and put on *Rumpelstiltskin* in 1922 and 1923, with incidental music by Mr and Mrs Salsbury. People were encouraged to attend the 'Theatre Royal, Leckhampton', in preference to 'that other village known as Cheltenham'. Other local theatre groups were emerging, and in 1927 the Leckhampton Gaiety Company gave two concerts in aid of the Children's Hospital Extension Fund and in 1930 there was mention of 'A Jolly Affair' performed by the Jolliwogs, 'who hide their identity under a name which so closely resembles that of a doll beloved by children'. (None of this would be countenanced today, of course.)

The string band of Mr W A Salsbury and the Misses Salsbury performed at a number of concerts and other functions. Later, at a service held in 1921 to raise money for the Memorial Chapel Fund parts were played by Dr Janet Salsbury, FRCO, Miss Edith Salsbury (violin) and Mr W A Salsbury ('cello). (In 1910 Janet Salsbury had been congratulated in the Parish Magazine on being the first woman to gain a Doctorate of Music at Durham University. In 1936 the family presented a new organ to the church.)

'Professor Du Cann – a very able Ventriloquist' was mentioned in 1898, when a mandolin trio and a *Bigotphone* Band also played. (The bigotphone is a simple wind instrument similar to the kazoo.)

The versatile G B Witts, after a lecture on 'Leckhampton and its neighbouring hills', sang some old Gloucestershire ballads, notably 'The stwuns [ie stones] that built George Ridley's oven'. On another occasion he gave a chat on Natural Science with 'tricks' and 'experiments of quite a startling character'.

Smoking Concerts

Some of the entertainments formed part of 'Smoking Concerts', In December 1898, it was reported that 'we mustered pretty well 100 pipes'. (Such concerts were widely popular, and in 1894 the *Church Times* had occasion to deplore a 'sacred smoking concert' held in Birmingham on Good Friday and presided over by a local vicar. Smoking Concerts survived as part of Oxbridge undergraduate life until more recently, but they surely would be frowned upon nowadays on health grounds.)

Tableaux Vivants

Tableaux Vivants represented well-known pictures, the actors being dressed in appropriate costume against a painted background and with musical or other accompaniment. Such entertainments continued well into the 20th century and will be remembered by some of those who took part. Examples are:

'Dante's Dream' (with solo violin)
'Sleeping Beauty' (with recitation from Tennyson);
'The Little Match Girl' (during which 'Ora Pro Nobis' was sung).

In 1920, during two consecutive evening performances, the tableaux represented the birth and childhood of Jesus. The report remarked on 'the reverence shown by the actors. The slightest sign of levity would have marred the effect of those sacred scenes.'

Not long after their formation in September 1925, the St Peter's Players put on a Nativity Play, which was preceded by two tableaux showing *The Virgin Mary at Nazareth* and *The Annunciation*. In 1932, the Young Men's Bible Class performed 'really beautiful Burmese tableaux in original dresses'.

Lantern Lectures

Lantern lectures and displays drew large audiences. In March 1896 Colonel Graham gave a lecture on 'Upper Burmah' with 'views through the Lantern – thrown upon the screen with the lime-light'. Colonel Graham also provided lantern views to illustrate a Good Friday evening talk on the story of the Passion, projected on to a special 'lantern sheet valance'. A lantern display for the school in January 1899 showed 'A Winter's Tale' and 'How Bill Adams won the Battle of Waterloo', and in 1902 the Reverend N Walsingham Gresley gave a lecture with lantern views on 'The Missionary Journeys of St Paul'.

The cast of the *Pied Piper* pantomime in the Parish Hall in 1909. Photograph from the *Cheltenham Looker-on, courtesy of Gloucestershire Libraries*

The cast of *Rumpelstiltskin* in 1922

Miss D Cotton (Rumpelstiltskin) and B C Enoch (Lord Never Saydie), Alf Bendall (Napoo the Tester), H Bendall (King Stoneybroke of Lackington), and Miss F Bendall (Duchess of Comme-il-faut).   Photo: *the late Terry Enoch*

The Jubilee Bonfire, 1897

Chapter Five

PEACE AND WAR

ROYAL AND OTHER STATE OCCASIONS

Queen Victoria's Diamond Jubilee

In 1897 Clifford Aston enthused over the arrangements in the parish to celebrate Queen Victoria's Diamond Jubilee, even though it was 'difficult to arrange matters, as five-eighths of our people are in the Borough of Cheltenham'. In June he wrote that 'the anniversary of the actual day of the Accession should call forth our deepest feelings .... The visit of H.R.H. The Prince of Wales to review the Yeomanry at Prestbury stirred the great majority of us, I believe, to go and help give him the hearty welcome he received, everyone, it seems, having had a good look at our future King.' (This took place in May – an occasion of pomp, as is shown in contemporary photographs of the Prince's party in front of the Pump Room and riding in procession to the Queen's Hotel.) When the celebrations were all over, Clifford Aston exclaimed:

'What a glad month it has been! Long will Wednesday, June 30th live in the memories of all of us. It was a splendid blaze on the hill on the evening of Queen's Day, and everyone so joyous and burning with loyalty and enthusiasm. Great credit is due to Messrs Sharpe and G Barrett for the skilful construction of the pile. 'Fairyland' is the only term that worthily describes the scene at Hill House when darkness set in. And I suppose not one of the large company assembled – the whole Parish almost to a man – but found keen enjoyment in the good fellowship and glad harmony that everywhere prevailed. Needless to say, the abundance of good things provided was much appreciated, to the strains of gentle music by the Town Band, and couples tripped it merrily on the green, and seemed incapable of fatigue.

'The ringers had been busy in the afternoon too, and gave touches of Grandsire doubles and Queen's changes, and fired the historic 'Sixty' in fitting honour of the occasion.' (In other words, all eight bells were struck simultaneously 60 times.)

'We shall not have done badly either in the way of permanent memorials of this great Reign. There is the Parish Hall for one – if only it was paid for! Then the Queen's Day saw the new Clock going – a great acquisition for the parish ... And another most useful present shortly to adorn the parish is the Drinking Fountain, presented by Mr and Mrs Taunton. Standing opposite the Malvern Inn it will prove a real boon to wayfarers, both four-legged and two. It is to be hoped that the Corporation of Cheltenham will give back freely through this source some of the water they take from the hill.'

The drinking fountain and troughs at the corner of Church Road.
They were removed in 1949.

Clifford Aston further records that Mr Walker, a churchwarden, presented to each schoolchild 'a very tastefully bound and well written book on the reign of Queen Victoria as they walked home for the Jubilee week's holiday. A copy turned up recently at the Red Cross Bookshop in Bath Road (illustrated opposite), but unfortunately, with no name in it.

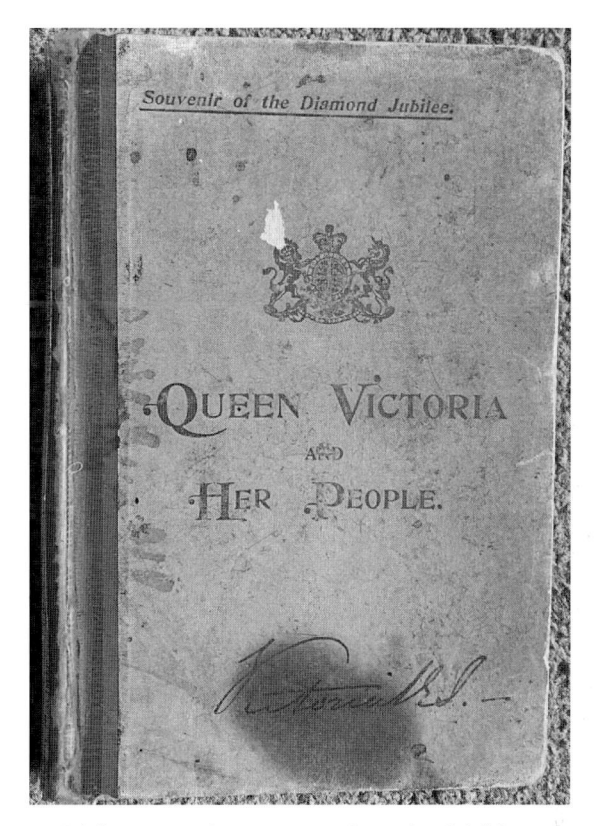

Jubilee souvenir, as presented to schoolchildren.
Courtesy Anne Gale

The Coronation of King Edward VII

In the summer of 1902 we learn of the postponement of Edward VII's coronation because of a 'critical operation' on the King. On the actual day (9th August), there was a 'hearty service' in the church at noon, and at 2 o'clock a dinner in the Parish Hall for all parishioners of the age of the King upwards (ie 60 and over). Then there were games in the field near the school, and at 4.30 p.m. all children up to the age of 16 residing in or attending any of the schools in the parish sat down to a 'meat tea'. At 6.30 p.m. Mrs G B Witts performed a ceremonial planting of the 'King's Oak' beside the Parish Hall (the tree had little chance of surviving). Finally there was dancing and 'kiss-in-the-ring', while fairy lights decorated the evergreens at the entrance to the field.

Mrs G B Witts planting 'the King's Oak', 9th August 1902

Empire Day, 1924

Another patriotic occasion was the celebration of Empire Day in 1924. 'At 9 a.m. the Union Jack was hoisted outside the School in the presence of the teachers, scholars, Chairman and Correspondent of the Managers and a few visitors ... Two verses of the National Anthem were sung (we had got tired of the 'Confound their politics' verse).'

The Death of King George V and Coronation of King George VI

By contrast with the lavish celebrations for Queen Victoria's Diamond Jubilee, King George V's Silver Jubilee in 1935 was a more restrained affair. 'Our parish is now almost entirely within the Borough of Cheltenham, and we shall not indulge in any particular celebration.' Thanksgiving services were nonetheless held, and loyalty pledged.

In February 1936, following the King's death, there was a one-page tribute, edged in black. Canon Sears, in a later review of that year, referred to 'the tragedy of the abdication' and regretted that a reign which began with such promise should have been brought to a close so prematurely. However, he believed that George VI and Queen Elizabeth would maintain 'the high standard which England has learnt by long experience to look for from occupants of the throne'.

When George VI was crowned in 1937, it was similarly decided that Leckhampton could not compete with the borough in its celebrations. However, the Coronation Committee provided entertainment for the older people, while the borough did the same for the schoolchildren. (Some readers may still have Coronation mugs from that occasion.) The residents of Pilley Crescent supplemented this by providing tea and entertainment in the Parish Hall, where Mr Charlesworth, Minister of the Baptist Chapel, made a short speech. The Coronation Committee ended with a surplus, which it decided to spend on a wireless set for the school, as a lasting memento of the Coronation. The Mayor of Cheltenham presented it, suitably inscribed, and said that while the main burden of teaching must always rest upon the staff the fullest use must be made of mechanical aids.

WARS

I. THE BOER WAR

Repercussions of the Boer War (October 1899 – May 1902) were felt both in the support provided by the village and in reports of the active service seen by three of its young men. These embrace tales of derring-do, hardship and pathos but are also noteworthy for their unconscious portrayal of attitudes of the time.

Contributing to the War Effort

In December 1899 it was announced that Miss Vavasour was 'collecting for the Soldiers' and Sailors' Families Association. Let us hope that Christmas may see the war ended and a righteous peace secured, and the full liberation of our fellow countrymen, and others, from their state of assigned inferiority in the Transvaal.'

Many fund-raising events were organised, and in one way and another the citizens of Leckhampton raised over £100 towards the War Fund. Mrs Meredith, busy as ever, this time as Secretary to the Leckhampton Knitting Guild, wrote that 'comforts' had been sent to the South Wales Borderers and The Royal Fusileers, and that the handkerchiefs and knitted articles (socks, mittens, chest protectors and scarves) had been divided between them. Each regiment would receive two large parcels, between 10 and 11 pounds in weight. Mrs Meredith reported that the colonel's wife from The Royal Fusileers had written to thank all the Leckhampton helpers:

> 'The mothers of our young knitters will be pleased to know that tickets were firmly attached to the articles knitted by the school children, giving the knitter's name and age: so the soldiers will see that little fingers in Leckhampton have done what they could ... I am still nearly £1 short of the sum required for 40lbs of tobacco for The Royal Fusileers, notwithstanding Mr Thompson's efforts, who has collected 16/8d in twopences for the Fund.'

Presumably the 'twopences' were from the school, of which Mr Barnard Thompson was headmaster.

Leonard Barnard

At a smoking concert held in aid of the War effort, the songs had a strongly patriotic ring: 'The British Lion,' 'Tight Little Island' and 'Let me like a soldier fall'. During the evening G B Witts spoke of L W (Leonard) Barnard, one of three young men from Leckhampton who had volunteered to fight. He was clearly a remarkable young man. He was born at Bartlow (now demolished) on Leckhampton Hill in 1870. He was educated at home by his father, R C Barnard, and was apprenticed to the Cheltenham firm of architects Middleton, Prothero & Phillott before taking up an appointment in London. There he was also captain of a company of the Church Lads' Brigade.

He volunteered as a private in the Artists' Rifle Corps, and was one of their crack shots, winning Lord Methuen's cup among others. He joined the Lord Mayor's City Imperial Volunteers and as a consequence was made a Freeman of the City of London before leaving for South Africa.

Later Parish Magazines quote from his many letters home. After landing at Cape Town, his unit had been sent by train to the Orange River. The inhabitants at the different stations met the train with fruit and good things for the men. At one place a school of pretty girls came to chat to them while they waited. They told them of the trouble they had with their Dutch Mistress, and the fights with the 'disloyal' Dutch girls. It was difficult for the soldiers to realise they were not out for a picnic. 'This, however, soon came to an end, the cakes and fruit being replaced by bully beef and biscuit, and not enough of that.' On another occasion

Leonard Barnard wrote 'from a coal truck en route to Pretoria, packed like sardines, and very ragged as to clothing, and bare in parts'. In August 1900 a letter was interrupted when his unit had to go out on a farm-burning expedition(!). A farmer's wife had allegedly been passing on information to the Boers; the British chivalrously 'brought the woman and children into Pretoria in state: with a Cape cart and four donkeys'.

The Leckhampton Church Lads' Brigade and Scouts, 1910
Leonard Barnard eighth from left, in forage cap

In November 1900 Leonard Barnard returned to an enthusiastic welcome in Leckhampton. A subscription dinner was held in his honour in the flag-draped Parish Hall, and when it was over, the tables were cleared away and more parishioners were admitted. Twenty members of his Church Lads' Brigade from Camberwell had also come down for the occasion, and they took a large part in the programme. Their fife and drum band played selections, and they gave 'a capital display of manual exercises'. It is further recorded that 'Mr G B Witts, as chairman of the Parish Meeting, and in that sense the civic head of Leckhampton (though he wears only an ordinary watch chain), made a characteristically genial speech, welcoming Private Barnard. The response of the hero of the evening was as modest as it was interesting.' The evening continued with songs by various contributors.

For the boys the celebrations continued over the weekend. They were put up in the schoolroom, and next morning marched to Bartlow for breakfast. Afterwards they were driven in brakes to Birdlip, to see the meet of the Cotswold Hounds. Then Mr and Mrs Dimmer gave them a dinner at Cotteswold. In the evening there were fireworks at Ferncliff, Mr Sharpe's residence, and a triumphal dance took place round a big bonfire, with Private Barnard on the boys' shoulders. On Sunday morning the boys duly attended church before returning to Camberwell, full of enthusiastic appreciation of their holiday.

George Yeatman

George Yeatman also set off for South Africa in early 1900. Aged 20, he had for three years been a member of the Cheltenham 2nd Volunteer Battalion, Gloucester Rifles, and was one of the Cycle Corps. He wrote in November 1900 of escorting Boer prisoners, 'a rough lot, not like our soldiers. Some had large bundles, and some carried umbrellas.' He also experienced the novelty of having baboons for company, playing round his fire with a cocoa can, and seeing a swarm of locusts for the first time.

Sidney Thompson

Sidney Thompson, the third volunteer, the son of the above-mentioned Mr Thompson, was serving with the Imperial Yeomanry and wrote from Aldershot in March 1901, thanking nearly 100 of his friends for their contribution of £6-17s-3d. In September 1902, Clifford Aston reported that Sidney had returned safely from the front, 'entirely recovered from the fever that attacked him'. A peal of bells was rung to welcome him home. (He would lose his life during the First World War, however.)

II. THE FIRST WORLD WAR

On Active Service

Regrettably, very few copies of the Parish Magazine have survived to shed light on the part played by Leckhampton during the First World War. Magazines must have been published during the period, however, since the volume for 1918 (the only one available) does not appear to have been limited in any way by wartime restrictions, and the run of St Philip and St James's magazines continued throughout.

Those listed as being on active service in July 1918 were Lieutenant Fenning (G Wilson Fenning, the Headmaster of Leckhampton School), Captain Leonard Barnard and Lieutenant Louis Sharpe (the military credentials of the two latter having been shown when in charge of the Church Lads' Brigade). Mr Harper, the organ blower, had also joined up.

The Reverend Austin Hodson, who in 1917 had offered his services as a chaplain, was still waiting the call in March of the following year. He knew that it was only a matter of time, and his brother from St Stephen's (the Reverend R L Hodson) was 'almost certainly going'. He saw no possibility of the war ending 'so long as there exists a large proportion of the nation who are indifferent to and refuse to acknowledge the Majesty of God'. His sisters would remain at the Rectory, as it was 'unthinkable that they should be uprooted as well'. The Reverend W H Peacey, of Tewkesbury Abbey, would attend to the parish in his absence.

At last, in August 1918, Austin Hodson was in France and wrote to his parishioners from there. He had 1500 people to look after, in two hospital camps. One was occupied chiefly by 'nerve' cases, the other by Chinese labourers. The choir had presented him with a knife, pipe and tobacco pouch engraved with his initials and a large Union Jack, which he spread on an old table in a tent that served for an altar.

In December 1918, still in France with the British Expeditionary Force, he wrote with relief of the victory and looked forward to peace, though he expressed anxiety about the influenza epidemic at home. His advice was that 'sicknesses of the epidemic variety, as all past experience goes to prove, find fewest victims where there is least panic and fear'.

Prisoners of War

In August 1918 'Prisoners' Day' was declared to raise money for food parcels to be sent to prisoners. There were three POWs from Leckhampton out of over 100 from Cheltenham as a whole. It was estimated that £400 was needed to meet the demands of the next 12 months, in sending each man four parcels a month, mainly of tinned food and weighing 16lbs. Mrs Cole at Dumfries House was said to have 'a veritable grocer's shop' in her basement, and received back acknowledgement cards in the men's own hands as proof of receipt.

There was 'abundant evidence that these parcels stand between our prisoners and starvation'.

Food parcels at Dumfries House ready for despatch to POWs
(*Inset*: Mrs Cole's mother, Mrs Elphinstone Shaw)
Cheltenham Chronicle & Graphic 3 March 1917

The Fallen

In February 1918 it was reported that Victor Frederick Alfred Hunt, a Private in the Royal Inniskilling Fusileers, had died of wounds in France the previous December. (He is commemorated by one of the three wooden crosses in the churchyard; the others are to Harold Summers and Alfred Enoch, M.M., both of the Glosters. The original crosses were brought back from France and dedicated on Armistice Day 1925; they eventually fell into disrepair and have since been replaced by more substantial ones.)

Other losses recorded in June 1918 included Charles Richings, RFA, of whom a friend wrote 'you will be glad to know he did not suffer'. Another soldier was unofficially reported missing, but after six weeks of suspense his parents heard from him, wounded and taken prisoner. Sergeant Cyril Lacey, killed in April 1918, had been an Assistant Master at the School for a short time until war broke out, and it was recalled that 'the roses in our school garden were struck by his hand'. Sympathy was extended to Sister Molly of the Leckhampton Court Red Cross Hospital, whose husband, Norman Wallis of the Australian Imperial Forces, had died in hospital in France from the effects of gas poisoning. Captain Maurice Desmond Quill, RMA, aged 22, after gallant active service and being mentioned in despatches, died from injuries in a riding accident on parade while at home on short leave. He was the elder son of Surgeon-General Quill of Leckhampton Lodge.

The deaths of the Boer War veteran Sidney Thompson and his brother Ernest would surely have been announced in one of the missing magazines.

Peace Celebrations

Following the Armistice on 11th November 1918, it was claimed that Leckhampton's bells were the first to have been heard in the Cheltenham district, after being silenced during the war. A Roll of Honour was placed in the church early the following year. (In 1985 this painted board was rediscovered in the Parish Hall by Jim Feather, who renovated it and restored it to the church.)

Austin Hodson was soon back in the Rectory and began to write of plans for memorials and celebrations. Two memorials were under consideration, a 'Parish memorial' and a 'Soldiers' Corner' in the church.

The Parish Peace Celebrations were held in August 1919, organised by Mr John Aston (brother of Clifford Aston) and Mr G Wilson Fenning. A reference to Mr Fenning's 'cleverly illustrated invitation card' reminds us that after his retirement as Headmaster he took up a career as a cartoonist (see David Webber's *The History of Leckhampton School*). There were sports for the youngsters, the Volunteer Band played, and the Cadena Cafe Company served tea and a dinner, at which Colonel Elwes (now promoted) gave a 'weighty' speech.

War Memorials

Leonard Barnard was asked to submit a design for the Village Cross, and by the autumn of 1919 it had been accepted and was on display in 'Mr Webley's window' – ie the Post Office, run by Frank Webley. (This drawing is reproduced overleaf.) The work was to be undertaken by the Leckhampton Quarry Company. The memorial was unveiled on Easter Monday 1920 by Sir Ashton Lister (MP for Stroud), and the lesson was read by the Reverend C H Robinson, Minister of Pilley Baptist Chapel. The surrounding holly hedge, which is still there, was planted at that time. The concrete and stone slabs which surround the memorial were placed there by Mr Alfred Bendall in 1926.

Leonard Barnard's impression of the proposed War Memorial

Separately, in the summer of 1920 an appeal was opened for a War Memorial to take the form of a chapel in the south aisle of the church, for which Leonard Barnard had drawn up plans. The effigy of Sir John Giffard and his lady (which until this time had been in the southeast corner, together with all the other memorials to the Lords of the Manor) was moved to the back of the church. The floor was paved with polished Leckhampton stone (peagrit and trigonyx in alternate squares), and a stone altar was erected.

The chapel – then generally known as 'Soldiers' Corner', now the Lady Chapel – was dedicated on 4th April 1921. It was also the intention to place a stone tablet in church listing the names of the fallen, but this was abandoned in favour of a book of remembrance. Made by Miss Beata Legh of Minchinhampton, its cover is of carved oak and the names and other details were written on vellum. (During the First World War centenary years the book was displayed in church together with a newly compiled Book of Remembrance. These are now on show in the glass-topped table in the Lady Chapel. The complete Book of Remembrance can be seen on the Local History Society's website.)

The carved oak cover of the First World War book of remembrance

The commemoration of Armistice Day in 1921 set the pattern for the years immediately following. It was observed on 11th November itself; its postponement to the following Sunday is a more recent practice. There was a service at church in the morning, with two minutes' silence – at the eleventh hour of the eleventh day of the eleventh month. This was preceded by the tolling of a bell, one stroke for each soldier on the memorial list. In the evening there was a procession to the Village Cross, at which a large crowd gathered, including Boy Scouts, Girl Guides and relatives of the fallen. Two mothers brought flowers to lay at the foot of the memorial. The Reverend C H Robinson was again involved, giving an 'earnest address', which was followed by a reading of the Roll of Honour, the Last Post and Reveille, and finally the ringing of a muffled peal of bells. In addition, in 1922 a newly acquired St George's flag was raised and dedicated on the flag pole beside the porch.

III. THE EVE OF THE SECOND WORLD WAR

In January 1939 the Rector, Canon Hensman, wrote of 'the world's troubled and troublous state' and urged parishioners to 'abstain from criticising other nations …. We must make our contribution to the scheme for voluntary National Service.'

Concern for the persecuted Jews was reflected in plans for a demonstration to be held in Cheltenham on behalf of the Refugees' Fund in January 1939, at which Mr D Lipson, the local MP, 'whose knowledge of the treatment of his own race is obviously intimate' was to have spoken, and 'an unknown refugee, whose personal experiences cannot fail to be poignantly interesting'. In the event, however, this meeting was cancelled, for reasons unstated.

During the glorious summer that preceded the outbreak of war many people took their last chance of normal enjoyment – the Mothers' Union outing and the Sunday School treat, for example. The church's missionary work continued, at least for a time, unaffected by the 'phoney war', and the Church of England Zenana Mission was still active in early 1940.

By the end of August 1939, Canon Hensman hoped that 'even at the eleventh hour common sense and common humanity will prevail and that we shall not be plunged into the horrors of war to satisfy the power-lust of dictators. The whole Empire will support the Imperial Parliament in its decision.'

After the declaration of war congregations at St Peter's remained 'consistently good ... the paramount importance of spiritual armaments is recognised'.

On Remembrance Day, 1939, the customary stopping in the streets and observance of the two minutes' silence at 11 a.m. were dispensed with 'for obvious reasons'. There were two services of Holy Communion as well as a short service at the War Memorial. At a service on the afternoon of the following Sunday, uniforms, medals and decorations were to be worn.

There were no Christmas bells that year at St Peter's – nor did they sound again anywhere in the country until the war was over; they were to be rung only in the event of invasion.

Canon Hensman's tenure of office came to an end in 1941. His successor, the Reverend Eric Cordingly, was away on active service and did not take up the post until after the end of the war, during which he was a prisoner of the Japanese. In the interim the parish was in the care of the Reverend Percy Unwin.

Chapter Six
THE CHURCH

THE CLERGY AND THEIR PREOCCUPATIONS

From the monthly letters and other contributions by the village parsons it is possible to build up a picture of their contrasting characters and concerns. They responded to the circumstances in which they were writing, but all shared a firmness in encouraging sound doctrine and conduct as well as regular attendance at church.

The Reverend Reginald Edward Trye was appointed Rector in 1884 but was obliged to leave the parish in 1895 as a consequence of his bankruptcy (associated with his family's disposal of the Leckhampton estate). From then until the year after his death in 1928 the parish was cared for by 'Curates-in-Charge'. Reginald Trye's early optimism, as shown in the letter quoted at the beginning of this book, contrasts with his farewell message. This refers to his close attachment to Leckhampton, in whose Rectory he had been born, and in whose church he was baptised and confirmed and had preached both his first and last sermons. He was buried in the churchyard in March 1928, aged 87.

The Reverend William Clifford Aston was Curate-in-Charge from 1895 until his death on 13th February 1904. He was probably the most influential person in fostering a sense of village community at the turn of the century. In a tribute to his memory, his mind was said to be 'ever full of new projects' and the Parish Hall, which he regarded as the centre of social life in the parish, was seen to stand as the embodiment of his wishes for his people and an abiding monument of his own work. The accuracy of this appreciation will be evident from the earlier chapters of this book.

In 1900 as an Easter Offering Clifford Aston was presented with a bicycle, with free wheel, which he 'much needed ... but even more I value the spirit of kindly sympathy and encouragement that prompted the gift'. (Some of today's parishioners may recall the parting gift of a bicycle to Canon George Smith, accompanied with similar warm sentiments.)

Canon Henry Proctor was Curate-in-Charge from 1904 to 1912. He set out his aims as being 'to raise the spiritual tone and to involve the laity more actively'. He explained the obstacles he had to face in his personal ministry, with an invalid wife, and he referred to his 'domestic bereavement ... I have had practically to lead the life of a widower'. It was therefore perhaps no wonder that he advocated 'a life of spiritual work and worship which alone can bring consolation under the sorrows of our pilgrimage here'. He was given to stoical quotations such as 'whom the Lord loveth, He chasteneth', and in his New Year letter of 1909 he wrote that 'God of His mercy has spared us to live another year together in the same parish'. He carried a walking stick, black with silver mounting, which he was apt to forget, and twice he made a request for its return after he had had left it in someone's house.

In one of his Christmas letters he said he hoped that the people of Leckhampton would not encourage children in the practice of carol singing at the doors of houses, since 'besides being too often grossly irreverent and even blasphemous, it begets in them the demoralising habit of begging'.

He regretted his lack of personal acquaintance and doubted whether the numbers attending Holy Communion were as large as they had been previously. Nor can he have had much encouragement from his parishioners. In the summer of 1908 he had invited all 225 communicants on the Electoral Roll to tea in the Parish Hall. Though fewer than 50 gave their regrets, only 96 turned up for the 170 teas that were provided. He was very much disappointed after his six years of teaching and ministry by the poor attendance at the Lenten services, 'which [did] not point to the prevalence of much devotion or self-denial in our midst'.

The Reverend Augustine (Austin) Hodson (1915-1921, and later the first Bishop of Tewkesbury) meant to leave no one in doubt that he had spiritual responsibility for his parish. Referring to the desirable new residences in Church Road, he commented: 'nearer the Church and farther from God', and when the Matrimonial Causes Bill was before Parliament in 1918, he expressed the view that if it became law, then 'it would scarcely be worth winning the war'.

In 1919, while still ministering as a padre to the troops in France, he wrote concerning church reform. He maintained that long-standing abuses remained unremedied, for example scandals in connection with patronage and appointments, endowments and salaries, the immovability of incumbents and antiquated forms of worship. Parliament, he said, knew and cared little about such matters, though Disestablishment was not the answer. In this article, he foreshadowed the creation of synodical government and other more radical changes to clergy remuneration that did not take place for another 60 years.

Austin Hodson invited his brother, the Vicar of St Stephen's, to write an article concerning reunion with the Nonconformists. He argued against it, in particular the interchange of pulpits, reciprocal intercommunion and episcopal re-ordination. Though he numbered some his best friends among the Nonconformists, he stressed that 'they, or their parents, left the Catholic Church because they could not accept some dogma, doctrine or practice of the Church ... We must wait for the clear guidance of the Spirit, or we shall be sure to make a mess of it.'

In 1921 Austin Hodson printed an account of a debate on the Ministry of Women held at a Diocesan Conference. Miss Lilian Faithfull (Principal of the Ladies' College) was quoted as having proposed that 'opportunity should be given to women (duly qualified and approved by the Bishop) to speak in consecrated buildings and to lead in prayer at other than the regular and appointed services of the church'. This resolution was carried by a large majority.

He put an individual slant on Lenten self-denial, observing in 1918 that 'if all Christian people observed the rule of fasting voluntarily, it would be possible to avoid compulsory rationing'.

The Reverend Francis Reginald Standfast (1921-1928) gave an assessment of his sermons after his first year in office. There had been, he said, 'too many of a 'scolding' nature ... I have given expression to divers disappointed hopes. I ought to have borne these in silence ... Let us start afresh with new hopes for the coming year.' In 1926 he was concerned that his visiting had got terribly into arrears, 'only don't let me waste your time, and mine, talking about the weather; let us speak of more spiritual things'.

His rules for Lent enjoined parishioners to give up public dances, whist drives and theatres and to 'do more solid reading and less of a light nature'. He believed that 'we ought not to spend too comfortable a Lent. It is meant to hurt us a little. The pain of Lent leads to the glory of Easter.' He did not regard Good Friday as a day for sport or play.

On another occasion he urged people to 'stop reading those soulless novels with their earth-bound, unspiritual ideals'. He was himself evidently a devotee of the writings of Dame Julian of Norwich, once requesting the return of her *Revelations of Divine Love*, which someone had borrowed.

It is no surprise that he did not approve of Jazz. He quoted an article on its evils, with an analysis of 'its effect on the morals of the white races ... a feverish exploitation of low types of pleasure in the younger generation'. The article linked the decay of great nations with the morality derived from their pleasures. 'Jazz is a low type of primitive music, in both structure and mode of performance. It is founded on crude rhythms ... it always puts emphasis on the grotesque by the banging and clanging of pots, pans or any shimmering metallic substance. It debases both music and instruments by making both farcical – the noble trombone made to bray like an ass, guffaw like a village idiot ... the essence of vulgarity.' F R Standfast invited anyone who thought he had a good defence of Jazz to send it in for publication. None was printed. Perhaps this article was printed as a consequence of the young people's pleasure at dancing to a jazz band, mentioned in Chapter 3.

F R Standfast was concerned over the industrial unrest in the aftermath of the First World War. In July 1921 he wished for 'more good news about the coal strike ... the adverse vote of the miners has come to dash our hopes'. He went on to speculate whether it was a result of the coal strike or some other cause that during the previous six months collections for special objects had fallen short. In 1925 he prayed for the industrial life of our nation, that those who preached class warfare, on either side, might cast out the spirit of revenge and suspicion. He was also conscious of 'the colour problem: if Christian faith and love prevail, that will solve itself, if not – race warfare!' He saw it as a hopeful sign that while in Africa the Prince of Wales had received communion from the hands of a black priest. 'God bless the Prince of Wales for that.'

On leaving the parish to become Vicar of Bracknell, F R Standfast quoted people as saying that they did not necessarily hold his church views but were really sorry that he was going. Nevertheless, he said that there was very little in his teaching that he regretted.

Shortly after his arrival in the parish **Canon Frederick William Sears** (Rector, 1928-1938) was asked by the Parochial Church Council to make an official statement concerning the incumbent's income and expenses, in view of the high cost of putting the Rectory and glebe buildings in order. His gross income was £837, of which rents from glebe land came to £500 and fees £300. Agent's fees, the rates of the church cottages, the upkeep of the churchyard, etc, amounted to over £129, and £1468 was required for renovation and repairs. As a consequence he would need a loan from the Queen Anne's Bounty, to be repaid at the rate of £240 per year. The net income was £467, about which F W Sears was not complaining. He merely wished to point out that it was not a 'fat living', and he regretted that he would be unable to contribute towards parish funds as liberally as he would have liked.

During the years of the Depression, in 1931, Canon Sears spoke of his anxiety about the country's financial condition and concluded that 'this serious threat to our national welfare and stability [is] a warning from God not to trust too much in the things of this world'. A General Election was imminent, which would be 'deeply responsible for shaping the future destiny of India and in furthering the cause of peace among nations at the forthcoming Disarmament Conference'.

Canon Sears was appointed Archdeacon of Cheltenham in 1932, remaining as Rector (a title which he said he would prefer parishioners to use) until 1938. Because of the rapid growth of the parish he spoke of the need of an Assistant Curate, if they could find the man – and the money. His prayers were soon answered, with the arrival of the Reverend T Teague, who had spent 20 years in the Diocese of Lebombo and Johannesburg. After two months, however, Mr Teague was forced to leave because of a sudden and unexpected change in the state of his wife's health. The Reverend F J Newth was appointed in his stead. To cover his stipend F W Sears asked the parish to raise at least £100, leaving £200 per year to come out of his pocket 'which is a much larger proportion than I can really afford to pay'.

CHURCH AND PARISH OFFICIALS

A number of church officials were thanked for their long years of faithful service. A few examples suffice to show the continuity and stability of the population:

Neighbour Pearman had been Parish Clerk for 45 years until a few months before his death in 1898 at the age of 68, apart from a period when he was Rector's Warden.

Nathaniel Smith, who died in 1903, aged 98, had been Rector's Churchwarden to Canon Trye for 25 years. His obituary recorded that 'there was never a scheme started for the good of the Parish, but Mr Smith was always a willing and able help. Many of the poor will miss a very kind friend. On the occasion of his funeral so many of his friends attended as well as others, of all classes.... He tried to live up to his name as Nathaniel, in whom was no guile.' (He built 'Wychbury', with its garden full of splendid trees and shrubs. He was also a founder of the Pharmaceutical Society of Great Britain.)

John Weaver, organist for over 31 years, was buried near the Vestry door in 1906.

Mr J F Ballinger resigned as Verger in June 1924 after 60 years of service.

William Henry Harrison died on 11th November 1934, aged 68. His address was 1 Church Cottages. (The cottages had been built originally for the express purpose of housing the Verger and the Sexton, according to Canon Sears.) He had been Verger and Sacristan since 1923, and also Sexton for much of the time until bronchitis forced him to give up outdoor work. His wife was listed as church cleaner. In his obituary,

Canon Sears gave him warm praise, paying tribute to his advice, 'flashes of humour and quaint remarks' and referring to his 'wonderful workshop'.

Reginald Read was appointed a server in August 1926. He still fulfilled those duties until shortly before his death in 1988. His late brother Fred also completed over 60 years as a server.

THE PAROCHIAL CHURCH COUNCIL

The creation of 'Church Councils' was encouraged in 1906, to reflect a more active concern on the part of the laity in the work of the church and to separate this from the conduct of secular affairs. In May 1906 a Register of Voters was drawn up, signed by 23 qualified electors (later on six more names were added), and for the time being these formed the Parochial Church Council. Both men and women were eligible (twelve years before women could stand for Parliament). The reason for the urgent convening of the Leckhampton PCC in 1906 is explained in the next chapter.

It was not until 1920, however, that the PCC became a legally recognised body by Act of Parliament. An Electoral Roll was drawn up in this connection, comprising 207 names out of the 450-500 who habitually worshipped. In 1935 Canon Sears commented that there were 'only 300 names on the Roll, though there were well over 400 communicants both at Easter and Christmas'.

CHURCH ATTENDANCE

Attendances at major services steadily rose during the latter years of the 19th century, with a growing population. At the Christmas Day services in 1897 there was a morning congregation of 68 communicants, 26 men and 42 women, which Clifford Aston described as 'encouraging – but I do not see anything like the number of our own village folk attending ... who might and ought to do so'. In the following year there were 83. The number of communicants at all three services on Easter Day rose from 76 in 1896 to 168 in 1903 (43 men, 123 women), and under Canon Henry Proctor, despite his pessimism, the numbers continued to increase, reaching 290 in 1909 and 1910. While figures have fluctuated considerably during subsequent years (see previous paragraph), recent (pre-covid) totals for Easter Day have been approximately 170 and 150 for Christmas Day.

SERVICES AND CEREMONIES

The Harvest Festival

While the Harvest Festival is still plays an important part in the church calendar, it and the state of the harvest in general will have meant much more to our predecessors, many of whom will have worked on the local farms or market gardens and will have understood the state of the crops. There was a setback in 1895, however, which prompted Clifford Aston to write:

> 'The only regrettable incident – for the thief, that is, who was so shameless – was the stealing of the grapes from the Holy Table and the robbing thereby of the sick people who would otherwise have enjoyed this little luxury. I don't believe for a moment that it was any of our people who could commit such a heathenish act.'

The grapes would otherwise have been taken to the Delancey Fever Hospital. In another year the Lady Superintendent of the Children's Hospital returned 'many grateful thanks for the large and acceptable truck of vegetable and fruit'.

In 1910 the Harvest Festival was held on a weekday in August, but arranged so as to enable as many as possible to attend: 7.30 a.m. Holy Communion, 9 a.m. children's service, 10.30 a.m. Morning Prayer, 11 a.m. Holy Communion and 8 p.m. Evening Prayer and sermon.

The Blessing of the Crops

The Rogationtide Blessing of the Crops was an equally important ceremony, which was held until the late 1950s. The participants would walk in procession from the church to the terrace of Leckhampton Court led by the Churchwardens, with cross-bearer, men and boys of the choir, the Rector, Sunday School, women and girls of the choir, the CEMS, the Mothers' Union, the Church Council, followed by the general congregation. In 1924 four banners were carried, one 'newly made for the use of the Mothers' Union at the great Mass Meeting in Cheltenham recently held ... and an interesting banner belonging to the Girl's Club', as well as others carried by the CEMS and Sunday School. A new Parish Banner was dedicated in 1937.

The Blessing of the Crops Procession, *c.* 1952
The cross is carried by Reg Read. The Rector is the Reverend Eric Cordingly, and
the choirboys include Derek Webb

Other Services

Confirmations sometimes alternated between St Peter's and St Philip and
St James's. As many as 30 – 40 candidates were put forward from St
Peter's in certain years.

The first celebration of Mothering Sunday, 'at any rate for a long
time,' was in 1928.

On Low Sunday in 1933 the Mayor and Corporation attended church.
Canon Sears commented that this had never happened before, as the
church was outside Cheltenham's boundaries, and the visit was due to the
fact that Captain Trye was Mayor.

THE CHURCH FABRIC

Stained Glass

The last three of the remaining plain windows were replaced with stained
glass at the beginning of the century. One of these was given by the
Baron de Ferrières in memory of his father, who had been buried earlier
at Leckhampton. The others were gifts of Mr Charles Hall and Miss
Swift.

Furnishings

In 1907 the brass lectern in the form of an eagle was given by Mrs Witts (the widow of Marmaduke Vavasour) in memory of her daughter Miss Caroline Vavasour, who had died the previous year.

In 1907 it was decided that it was undesirable for any further monuments to private individuals to be erected inside the church. (There was little enough room on the walls. Nevertheless, two further tablets were erected later, of which one, in the Lady Chapel, commemorates G B Witts and his wife.)

There were other opportunities for benefactions, however. Although no magazines are available for 1913, they would certainly have mentioned that a new pulpit, designed by L W Barnard, had been erected in memory of Mary Trye and Mrs Eleanor Meredith. According to an article in the *Cheltenham Looker-On* it was made of oak grown on the Leckhampton Court estate and was executed by Messrs Boulton and Sons.

In 1930 electric lighting was installed, paid for by Miss Ferryman in memory of her parents, General and Mrs Augustus Halifax Ferryman.

In 1935 a silver box for altar breads was presented by a married couple who, as boy and girl, had been confirmed 50 years previously and had since been regular communicants.

THE ORGAN

The 'wonderfully generous gift' of a new organ in 1936 by Mr Salsbury and his two daughters, Mrs Peebles and Dr Janet Salsbury, is duly recorded. *The History of Leckhampton Church* gives details of the specification.

In an earlier era there had been a need for an organ blower, who earned 2 guineas a year in 1902, rising to £2 a quarter in 1922; the last time that the position was specifically mentioned in the accounts was in 1923.

In 1901 Mr Dale donated a harmonium, for use at choir practice. It was still in use in 1907.

THE BELLS

In 1904 the Misses Richardson were thanked for the gift of two new bells, given in memory of their mother. For many years afterwards (at least until 1930) a commemorative peal was rung either on the date of their dedication in April or of Mrs Richardson's death in November.

It was a custom of the bellringers to ring a 'date touch' on special occasions. For example, 1901 changes were rung in memory of Mrs Harriet Arkell Hall when she died in that year.

Leckhampton Bellringers, *c*.1904

Standing, L to R: W Townsend, W Harrison, Arthur Caudle, Jack Shill, Alfred Pratt (Fred), Noah Newton. Alfred Hunt (always called Richard).
Seated: William Harley, Tom Hunt.

THE CHOIR

In 1907 the choirboys were said to be giving their services freely without the quarterly payment that had been the custom till then. They were however offered the promise of an outing if they attended regularly and punctually. Payment must have been reintroduced, for in 1919 they received a rise, which recognised that it was 'more than a privilege' to sing – three times on Sundays plus two practices during the week. The new scheme entailed putting on one side half of a choirboy's pay, which would be given to him on leaving, 'provided that he left satisfactorily'. Some boys were paid 12 shillings a quarter, some 8 and some (the least experienced, presumably) only 6 shillings. Collections at the Dedication Festival would go towards the outing. The church accounts show that this practice continued into the 1930s.

THE CHURCHYARD

In 1907 L W Barnard was said to have been preparing, with assistance from G B Witts, a plan of the churchyard. The area has been extended to the south since then, in 1935 and in 1948-50. (The finished version of the plan, dated 1914, is lodged with the County Archives. An updated copy is kept in the vestry, while members of the Leckhampton Local History Society and Gloucestershire Family History Society have transcribed many of the tombstone inscriptions and photographed the plots. These details are available of the Local History Society's website.)

Early in the 20th century it was evidently the custom to place 'glass shades' over some graves. That practice was forbidden in 1907, as they were constantly getting broken, causing danger and interfering with the cutting of the grass. In 1934 the PCC was concerned over the appearance of many of the grave mounds. It was threatened that if the relatives could not keep them tidy it would be better to level to the mounds.

Rights to Burial at St Peter's

The parishioners of St Philip and St James's traditionally had the right to burial at St Peter's, but this clearly rankled those who worshipped at the mother church, and Clifford Aston protested that 'in the circumstances those from the neighbouring parish really ought to help the Churchyard Fund'. In 1906 the right was restricted to those who had lived within the parish of St Peter's, but after a time that fact appeared to have been overlooked. In 1937 St Peter's PCC restated the ruling in a form of words which nevertheless would allow the burial of a non-parishioner, provided that the appropriate fees were paid. (A letter on the subject, written by the Vicar of St Philip and St James's, was published in the magazines of both parishes.)

COLLECTIONS AND CHARITIES

Local Welfare

The parish had a long-established responsibility for relieving local cases of hardship. We find one of the last reminders of this in a report of the Annual Parish Meeting in 1904, when Frank Hicks and William Restall were elected Overseers of the Poor, and John Weaver (the Organist – see above) Assistant Overseer.

Within the realm of ecclesiastical responsibilities, an Alms Committee allocated charitable funds and assistance. In 1907 it disbursed nearly £40. Its policy was not to attempt to relieve cases of chronic poverty 'nor where assistance would be likely to encourage thriftlessness', but rather to give substantial help in cases of special emergency, for example in time of sickness or following a death in the family. Two dozen aged persons and widows received special help during one winter. Assistance was given in paying rent, providing milk, coal and food, sending convalescents to the seaside or arranging special nursing. Boots and spectacles might also be paid for. The Eleanor Thorp bequest of 1902 was designed to provide coals and warm clothing for the poor of the parish. The committee would consider help to promising children who wished to enter the teaching profession or take up an apprenticeship and would assist young men or women emigrating to the colonies. A suitable outfit of clothing would be given to girls or boys leaving home for service. Two fully equipped 'Dorcas' boxes were also available free for the use of poor women at the time of their confinement.

A supplementary source of assistance was a 'Discretionary Fund', which derived its revenue from week-day collections, from complimentary fees at weddings and burials and from churchings of women after childbirth (a ritual which was regularly advertised until comparatively recently) as well as from special donations.

In 1918 the District Visitor reported that over 80 tickets for milk, groceries and meat had been given for varying lengths of time. The vouchers also covered hospital treatment and dentures, railway fares and cabs for patients.

Envious Gossip

The dispensing of such charity almost inevitably led to envious gossip in the village, over which Austin Hodson voiced his concern. He had been told that people went to church 'to get the Christmas coal'. While dismissing this accusation, he asked to be told immediately of any cases of illness or neglect in order to forestall blame for any possible oversight. Gossip similarly worried his successors. No doubt for some good reason, F R Standfast wrote an article describing 'ill-natured gossip, whether by word or letter' as 'a poisonous miasma, or an infectious disease, destroying all peace and charity, corrupting both him who speaks and him who listens'. Canon Sears in his turn had occasion to raise this subject, writing that he received annually a crop of anonymous letters about the time of the distribution of the Coal Charity, besides occasional specimens that arrived at other times. However, he said, he took no notice of their contents – anonymous letters went straight on the fire. If there were any facts which he ought to know, he asked people to come forward and tell him in confidence, so that he might take steps to find out whether there was any justification for the statement made. 'To write an anonymous letter in order to defame another person,' he wrote 'is like stabbing someone in the back.'

The Free Will Offering Scheme

The Free Will Offering scheme was introduced in 1918 and gradually became the backbone of parish finance, ensuring a steady income throughout the year at a time before covenants made it possible for charities to claim back tax on giving. To encourage participation in the scheme, in 1934 Canon Sears pointed out that there were no pew rents at Leckhampton, 'though in most, if not all, Cheltenham churches there is such a system', and in the circumstances suggested that members of the congregation put an equivalent amount into the FWO scheme. The absence of pew rents had been remarked on in 1906, when subscriptions to Church Expenses (in lieu of pew rents) came to over £50.

Old Age Pension Certificates

As the state gradually began to take over responsibility for aspects of welfare which the parishes (whether civil or ecclesiastical) could not hope to cover, Henry Proctor said in 1908 that he had received applications from various parts of the country for Old Age Pension Certificates (presumably a certificate of baptism to enable the person to apply for a state pension). He quoted one letter which was accompanied by a request for a view of 'thee Little Church ... pleas will you accept thes Few Cappers (4 stamps) For thee poor Box sory i cannot aford more i am only a poor widow'.

Missionary Giving

The parish gave (as it still does) to a wide range of charities at home and abroad. Some are well known today but others may be less familiar: missions to Borneo, Corea (*sic*), Melanesia, Mongolia, North China, Zululand, the Cambridge Mission to Delhi and the Oxford Mission to Calcutta. Closer to home, the Bussage House of Mercy was listed.

The East London Fund for the Jews featured conspicuously. On Good Friday in 1897 a limelight service was held in the Parish Hall in aid of the Jews' Society, at which the story of the Passion was illustrated with some pictures by Old Masters. In 1936 a Palestine Exhibition was held at Cheltenham Town Hall, under the auspices of the Church Missions to the Jews. Exhibits included a real 'tent of hair' purchased from a Bedouin tribe.

In 1900 a Missionary Loan Exhibition was publicised, to be held at the Winter Gardens. It was hoped that this would 'do something to rouse us to fresh effort in meeting the spiritual needs of the heathen and Mahometan world'.

The Church of England Zenana Missionary Society was a cause to which the parish gave regularly. It worked among women chiefly in India. In 1934 the Society held an exhibition in Cheltenham Town Hall, where nine 'courts' illustrated everyday life and the work of the society in schools and hospitals in India, Ceylon and China.

In 1920 there was an appeal for the leper children who were being looked after by a community of nuns on Robben Island, off Capetown. (The island gained notoriety in more recent years as the prison which housed Nelson Mandela and other opponents of Apartheid in South Africa.)

In 1930 the parish promised £10 per year towards the stipend of the Rector of Narembeen parish in Western Australia. It was described as a small town of about 50 houses, where mostly wheat was grown, but several bad seasons had hindered its development. The Rector was living in a hostel and used the vestry of the wood and iron church as a study. The average congregation at evensong was 20; it was held at 7.30 p.m. to enable people playing games to attend at least one service.

The 'Russian Relief Fund'

In November 1921, in the aftermath of the Russian Civil War, F R Standfast wrote that all through the Harvest Thanksgiving thoughts were with 'our starving fellow Christians in Russia ... and still we continue to pray that that stricken land may have better days'. The substantial amount of £32 was collected for their assistance. In 1926 he reminded readers that the atheistic government of Russia was trying to kill the Church, but the gates of Hell would not prevail. Meanwhile he asked for contributions to an Academy for Russian Clergy in Paris.

Christians in Iraq

A fund for Assyrian Christians in Iraq was opened in 1925. This remnant of the old Assyrian Church had fled to avoid massacre by the Turks and taken refuge in the then British mandate of Iraq. (Similar persecution has since befallen Iraqi Christians living under the rule of Saddam Hussein and even more recently under Isis terrorism.)

Human Sacrifice

In connection with an appeal for funds in 1935 for the Jane Furse Hospital in South Africa, a letter from the Bishop of Pretoria was printed. Headed *Human Sacrifice Today*, it described an episode which took place not far from the hospital. There was a graphic description of the killing, disembowelling and dismembering of a young boy under the direction of a witch-doctor, who had ordered the sacrifice to bring rain. The police had found out and investigated and arrested the murderers, but a few days later a tornado struck the police post where they were being held, which was interpreted as being the witch-doctor's snake trying to release them. It did rain soon afterwards, as the incident occurred near the start of the rainy season. Canon Sears commented that 'it is difficult to conceive that anyone, after reading the article, could ever say that the African has a religion which is suited to him and that we ought to leave him to it and not attempt to convert him to Christianity'.

'Borneo Boy'

One of the most curious and enduring objects of charitable giving was 'Borneo Boy'. In December 1919 Austin Hodson wrote that he proposed to use the Sunday School offering 'to help support a 'brown baby' in Borneo ... a little Dyak, for our very own'. They were promised a little boy by the name of 'Kit', but in March they learned from the Borneo Association that there were no 'babies' and that 'Kit' seemed to be a figment of the imagination. Instead, the parish was to take care of a fully grown boy called Gian Tian Swee, aged 13. He was a pupil at St Thomas's School, Kuching, where the annual fee for his education was

£12. By 1921 Gian Tian Swee had written to say that he was a choirboy at the cathedral and also an altar-server. Collections were still being made for him in 1926. The following year contributions went to a Girls' School in Betong.

By the 1930s Gian Tian Swee had been succeeded by Beng Hap, who in 1936 obtained a job as a dresser in the Government Hospital. The next to benefit was Lin Ban Sing, a promising scholar whom the Principal was hoping to be able to send to Hong Kong to train as a doctor. 'He is a very religious lad and hopes when he qualifies to be able to devote his life not only to the curing of the bodies of men but also to the work for and with the Church in the conversion of the people of Sarawak.'

In the 16 years during which the Sunday School supported the Borneo Mission it had given a total of £210, of which was £160 in scholarships to St Thomas's School and £50 went towards the building of St Margaret's Girls' School, Betong.

Collections towards Local Hospitals – 'Hospital Egg Days'

An unusual means of raising funds for Cheltenham's hospitals that began during the First World War was the annual collection of eggs one day in springtime. This practice continued until at least the late 1930s. Leckhampton was always keen to achieve the highest total. In 1918 5000 eggs were collected, of which Leckhampton's contribution came to £278, plus £1-18s-11d in cash. Following the end of the war there was no further demand at the Red Cross hospitals (such as that at Leckhampton Court) and support was therefore directed to the General Hospital.

In 1921 an item read: 'Eggs! Eggs! Eggs! Wednesday April 14th. Mrs Delmar-Williamson has undertaken to have a receiving depot at Firs Lodge, Moorend Road. The Hospital hopes to get 10,000 eggs.' Leckhampton hens managed to produce 602 eggs, and in successive years the village consistently increased its total, peaking at 1160 in 1928; 800 eggs were collected in 1932 plus 299 pennies, of which the school contributed 226 eggs and 36 pennies.

Probably an annual event was a Hospital Pound Day, whose beneficiaries included the Eye Hospital and the children at St Monica's Home ('Waifs and Strays'), Battledown Approach, where the villagers also supported the 'Leckhampton cot'. In 1924 the subscription list included the names of 36 lady parishioners plus the Leckhampton Quarry Company, which made the largest contribution, of 2 guineas.

THE SUNDAY SCHOOL

The Sunday School was a sizeable undertaking, with as many as ten classes in 1899. It occupied the Parish Hall in the afternoon, while Boys' and Girls' Bible Classes were held in private houses. By 1909 the Sunday School had both Lower and Upper Schools plus a Bible Class for the oldest children. The Lower School, for ages 3 – 9, was taught by four teachers according to 'the Kindergarten system, which aims at enlisting the activities of eyes and hands to help the intellect'. The Upper School, superintended by Miss Proctor, catered for those aged 9 – 14 and was divided into classes of eight.

In the mid-1930s the pupils numbered 170, and an Old Members' Club was formed, with over 40 members initially. There were only four teachers to 64 children in the senior department, and more were needed.

In 1935 the teachers were provided with weekly training by Miss Knollys, the Junior Sunday School Superintendent. This included a 'Black Board Demonstration' by Miss Wilson of the staff of Cheltenham Ladies' College. (Miss Knollys was probably Miss M E Knollys, herself the former Head of the Ladies' College Kindergarten.)

EMMANUEL CHURCH

In 1928 a Diocesan Commission recommended that a permanent church should be built in Emmanuel parish, to replace a building in Naunton Terrace. It was also considered that there was a probable need of a new church in the Old Bath Road neighbourhood, 'for which an excellent site has been procured for £1400' (the actual location was not given).

An appeal was opened for the erection of a new building for Emmanuel in June 1936, though Archdeacon Sears commented that people were 'not very sympathetic towards the scheme'. However, the Bishop of Gloucester wrote: 'That the church is needed, no one acquainted with the parish can have any doubt. There are some 5000 people, largely of the working classes, and the present temporary building is unsuitable. Moreover, there is no Parish Room. The parish has to rent one, and the rent is being increased.' Construction must have been quick, for the foundation stone was laid in October 1936 and the consecration of the new church was performed in October 1937. Archdeacon Sears added that 'our neighbours will at last have a suitable building in which they may worship'.

Chapter Seven
THE SCHOOL

THE VILLAGE SCHOOL

The activities of the village school were regularly reported in the pages of the magazine. As a 'National School' (ie functioning under the aegis of the National Society for promoting the Education of the Poor in the Principles of the Established Church), it relied upon the local ecclesiastical authorities to provide and maintain the buildings.

Enlarging the School

The school had three stages of development during the period in question: the original 1841 building, a new school for juniors built in 1906 and one for infants built in 1931.

Schoolchildren with their teacher outside the original school, *c.* 1890

The New School, 1906

In April 1904 Canon Henry Proctor reported that the existing building and its little yard were considered unfit to accommodate the number of children who wished to attend. (The estimated cost of a new building was £4500, a debt which was eventually paid off in 1908.) Mrs Nevile Wyatt (patron of the living and mother-in-law of the Reverend Clifford Aston) made the offer of an acre of land on which to build the extension, and the momentum quickly grew. The Bishop of Gloucester laid the foundation stone on 3rd July 1905. There was every prospect that the school would be ready for Easter 1906, but an unexpected delay prevented the building from being occupied until the following September. It is worth recounting the reasons, which have echoes in our own time.

The delay was in protest against a new Education Bill which was then before Parliament. On 24th April the Parochial Church Council (hastily convened to deal with the emergency) discussed the Bill and passed unanimously a resolution that it 'so violates the principles of both religious and civil freedom ... that it must be met by the most strenuous opposition'. On 30th April, in what looks like a gesture of assertion on the part of the church authorities, it was the Rural Dean, Canon Roxby, who performed the dedication of the new school and not Alderman George Norman, as had evidently been planned.

Three worthies outside the newly built school, 1906.
Mr J D Bendall, the builder, Mr H W Chatters, the architect, and
Mr B G Thompson, the schoolmaster. *Cheltenham Chronicle and Graphic*

The new school, opened April 30, 1906
Cheltenham Chronicle and Graphic

At a meeting which followed the dedication, Canon Proctor spoke to parents about the 'arbitrary and unfair proposals of the Government Bill, which makes it impossible ... for us to offer the building to the Local Education Committee for the present to be used as a Day School'. He later wrote of the Government as 'threatening to forbid our children being taught the religion of their parents in their own schools, unless we can persuade the children out of school hours to come and receive it, and can find teachers ... to give it ... May God defeat this plot.'

It was not only in Leckhampton that there was opposition, of course. Readers were invited to attend a protest demonstration in Cheltenham Town Hall, chaired by Mr William Hicks-Beach, with addresses by the Bishops of Birmingham and Gloucester. Overflow accommodation would be provided in the Winter Garden.

The difficulty was eventually resolved. Canon Proctor reported that the new school would open on 3rd September 1906 for all children over three years of age. 'God defeated the plot in a marvellous way,' and the Trust Deed had been drawn up in such a way that guaranteed the teaching of religious education, even if the Bill were to become law (which in fact it did not).

There were, however, rumblings of discontent – described as 'civil war' at one point – from those parents who wanted 'undenominational' teaching for their children. A Parents' League was set up, with the aim of determining what religious teaching their children should receive in the schools to which they were obliged to send them; this league was still in existence in 1908. They were 'astounded to find a few of our friends from the chapel' who opposed what was being offered. An earlier hint of what must have been a continuing source of conflict had been evident in connection with the 1902 Education Act, which led to both 'board' schools and church schools being placed under one local authority. Clifford Aston wrote similarly of 'the bitter struggle over the religious difficulty' and the 'Nonconformist grievance'.

The New Infants' School, 1931

By 1929 the Local Education Authority considered the Infants' School building (the original school of 1841) to be no longer suitable; moreover, they would soon have to cater for children from 109 new houses to be built at Pilley. The Church Council drew up a proposal to build a new Infants' School. After August 1930 the school as a whole would become a Junior Mixed School, taking children only up to 11 years of age.

The final cost of the building was £2274-7s-1d. Although the Diocesan Board of Finance gave some assistance, the money was largely raised through sustained local voluntary efforts which culminated in a concert held in October 1933.

The infants were able to occupy the new building after the Whitsun holiday in 1931. The classrooms were described as 'light and airy, whatever people might think of the appearance outside' (the roof had attracted particular criticism). Inside, the teaching must have been good, for that year nine out of 23 candidates won full Scholarships to the Grammar Schools, eleven part Scholarships and one a pass. (It was not stated how many were boys and how many were girls.) In 1937 the Diocesan Inspector reported that the school was one 'of which the Church may well be proud in every way. The really good buildings are a great help, but the most important thing is the tone of the school which is just what it should be. The children have been very well taught and a good foundation is laid among the smallest ones.'

In 1935 some had expressed a wish to repair the old Infants' School with a view to turning it into a Young Men's Club or Institute. The Rector questioned whether there was really such a demand, and nothing further came of the idea.

FROM THE LOG BOOKS

In 1919 the Reverend Austin Hodson came across the old school log book which began in the early 1860s, and he saw that it could throw light on local history. He recounted how strawberry picking, potato planting, gleaning beans, and the hay harvest would half empty the school when the seasons came round, as many children helped their parents, many of whom were small market gardeners. So-called 'club feasts' also interfered with attendance and were a source of bitter rivalry and recrimination between Church and Chapel. Legitimate extra holidays were declared too, for such events as the review of the Yeomanry or the Curate's marriage; on another occasion the day was being kept as a day of humiliation on account of the Cattle Plague.

The Prizegiving in the Parish Hall on 22 December 1897 was typical of the period. Mr and Mrs Walker presented the prizes – a book for everyone who had attended 390 times, plus a shilling to the four scholars who had attended every time the school was opened – 405 half-day sessions.

The School Bank received deposits on Monday mornings, 9 – 9.30, and the Provident Society payments were made in the Schoolroom, 12 noon – 12.30 p.m.

Some more advertisements from the 1920s

POSTSCRIPT

Such was Leckhampton during the period from the end of Queen Victoria's reign to the eve of the Second World War. More could have been said, but within this little book there is enough to convey the intended impression. Producing it has been not simply an exercise in nostalgia, for it is only by knowing our heritage that we gain a true understanding of the present state and of ourselves.

Now that the book is written, I am satisfied that it was right to use the parish magazines as the prime source. In the absence of a truly local newspaper for Leckhampton, nothing could approach the magazine – aptly titled *The Messenger* for part of its existence - for advance notice, factual reports and comment on happenings both everyday and of wider import. Even for the somewhat more recent period of which some of our older inhabitants may have some experience, there is no substitute for a reasonably objective printed record of events. If this book prompts others to seek out hidden treasures of their own, then that will be an added achievement.

It would have been tempting to include more information taken from the parish magazines of St Philip and St James, St Peter's one-time daughter church, though long since fully fledged. Certainly there are many parallels and a degree of overlap between the activities of their parishes, but the two communities were and remain distinct, and I did not wish to dilute the vividness of the picture of life 'further up the hill'.

I am grateful to the Leckhampton Local History Society for publishing this book. Its other issues include *Leckhampton 1894 – the End of an Era, Leckhampton in the Second World War, Britain in Old Photographs – Leckhampton*, and five *Research Bulletins* with members' articles on a wide range of topics, including personal reminiscences. In 2018 a play based on material from the magazines – *Beneath the Devil's Chimney* – was read at one of its meetings, to great acclaim.

Eric Miller has served on the committee of Leckhampton Local History Society since its foundation and is currently its Co-ordinator of Research. Since his retirement from the Civil Service he has spent much of his time investigating the history of Cheltenham and its environs. He has written books on the history of the church and the court and, together with other members of the society, brought out *Leckhampton in the Second World War*. In 2000, together with Alan Gill, he edited *Britain in Old Photographs – Leckhampton*, which gained them an award from the Cheltenham Arts Council. He has also had numerous articles on local history published in a number of periodicals, including the journal of the British Association for Local History.

He first came to live in Leckhampton in 1959 and since 1969 he and his family have been closely involved with activities at St Peter's. He has served on the Parochial Church Council and was its Honorary Secretary from 1978 to 1981.

Leckhampton Local History Society was founded in 1992. Its aims are to collect, study and publish information concerning the history of Leckhampton and to stimulate public interest in local history. Meetings are normally held once a month in the Glebe Cottages, next to Leckhampton churchyard, for talks and discussions. Outings and field trips are also organised and there are opportunities to participate in research. Membership is over 100. Subscriptions include free delivery of *Smoke Signal*, the Society's newsletter, and entitle members to purchase certain Society publications at concessionary rates.

The Society's web address is www.llhs.org.uk